Man Creatures

How God Used Both His Spoken Word and Evolution to Create Man

DANIEL R. WILLIAMSON

PublishAmerica
Baltimore

First printing

At the specific preference of the author, PublishAmerica allowed this work to remain exactly as the author intended, verbatim, without editorial input.

ISBN: 1-4241-4057-9
PUBLISHED BY PUBLISHAMERICA, LLLP
www.publishamerica.com
Baltimore

Printed in the United States of America

Dedication

I dedicate this book to my wife, Kathleen Williamson, who is my gift from God. Without your unselfishness and incredible hard work, this book would not have been completed. Thank you for sticking in there with me.

Acknowledgements

I would like to thank my wife, Kathleen Williamson, for her skillful and creative work in the creation and typing of this book. Also thanks to her for her generous support during the preparation and completion of this book.

Table of Contents

Introduction

Mankind evolved from ape-like creatures by chance and necessity.

With the dust of the earth and His spoken Word, God supernaturally created mankind.

These two statements seem to completely contradict each other. The same can be said about the Book of Genesis found in the Bible and scientific evidence.

Could any two explanations for our beginnings be further from agreement? It seems it would take a miracle to reconcile scientific evidence with God's Word. When I consider how long mankind has been searching for understanding of Genesis, which is actually not in conflict with scientific evidence, I am left with little doubt that a miracle has taken place.

This book is about God's miraculous revelation of Genesis to mankind. After you read this book, the way you think about the world will change. My goal is to demonstrate how God created the universe and everything in it, including man, supernaturally by His spoken words and naturally through evolution.

About seventeen years ago, I came to a crossroad in my life. Deep inside, I needed to know if God was real or if He was only a crutch for weak-minded people. I started searching the Bible for answers.

I did not get very far in my quest to find the truth about the reality of God when a problem the size of a mountain formed in my mind. In an effort to solve this problem, I searched for seventeen years to find the answer to one question: If God is real and was the creator of the universe and everything in it, why doesn't the biblical story of

Genesis agree with scientific evidence concerning the formation of our universe, evolution, and man's origin?

Truly, I wanted to believe in the truthfulness of the Bible, but without reconciling the biblical story of creation with scientific evidence and the theory of evolution, I lacked faith in the Bible. However, after praying, seeking, and meditating for many thousands of hours, I have become convinced that the biblical version of creation and the scientific version of creation are actually the same story. Lack of true understanding about God's written Word has kept this information secret until now.

There is a great need for knowing the truth about Genesis. Every fall, millions of young Christians leave home in pursuit of higher learning. The sad fact is that too many of them lose their faith in God after being presented with overwhelming scientific evidence contrary to what they have learned in church. Maybe it is time to stop blaming educators and give our young people the information their hungry minds need to keep their souls safe.

Not all of us have young people living in our homes, but each of us will, someday, have to answer for the deeds we have done here on earth. Every day multitudes go to their graves not believing in God because the story of Genesis is not compatible with scientific evidence. Scientific knowledge, intelligence, and commonsense do not allow many to believe biblical explanations that are not scientifically sound. Believers need to know the truth about Genesis, but nonbelievers need it even more.

Have you a desire for a deeper understanding of creation? This book was written for those who know in their hearts that there is a God who is the power and intelligence that created the universe, but know in their minds that evolution is a fact of life. We will probably never know exactly how many Christians are torn by their beliefs because many will not want to admit to them. This book is for people with wisdom, commonsense, faith in God, and the courage to seek the truth.

On Day Six of creation, God spoke three "Let there be" statements, which created man in the image and the likeness of God the Father, God the Son, and God the Holy Spirit. Later God formed man as a soul, made him a living soul, and placed him in the Garden of Eden.

Today we live here on the physical earth and our bodies are a product of evolution. We have 99.9 percent of the same genes as an ape, which means our bodies evolved from a distant relative of apes.

This book will make sense regarding man's journey from God's spoken words found in Genesis 1:26, which created man in the image and in the likeness of God, to our present condition here in the earth.

There are a couple of problems that need to be addressed before reading this book. The first is pride. We cannot receive revelations, or higher understanding, if we are too proud to lay aside old beliefs.

There were many good, God-fearing Jews who could not believe that Jesus was the Christ sent from God, His Father. I believe it was pride that kept them from this belief. They had pride, not in the written Word, but in their understanding of the written Word.

One belief the Jews held was that the Messiah was going to set up a physical kingdom here on earth immediately upon His arrival. Their interpretation of the Torah, or Pentateuch, was wrong, and hanging on to this wrong belief cost them the opportunity to receive the very thing they wanted most, which was to obey God's will and to receive salvation.

All is not lost for the Jews however. Sometime in the future, God will save His Jewish people, whom he loves greatly.

> And so all Israel shall be saved: as it is written, There shall come out of Zion the Deliverer, and shall turn away ungodliness from Jacob:
>
> Romans 11:26

What do you believe? Are you willing to trade your old understanding for the deeper meaning of God's Word? The price for deeper understanding is pride.

God's Word is truth. Understanding of the written Word belongs to each of us. Sometimes we overlook the deeper meanings within the Scriptures. Having opinions about what is written and sharing this understanding is very good, but confessing that one's own understanding is the *only* truth is wrong, very wrong.

When digging deep for biblical secrets, the tool of choice is an open mind. Open your mind now and prepare for a journey to deeper understanding.

Author's Note on Biblical References

All Bible verses quoted in this book come from the Authorized King James Version of the Bible. For many years, I used every version of the Bible that I could get my hands on. This practice confused me on several occasions. In my spirit I didn't feel right using so many different versions of the Bible. I felt that I was trying to make God's written Word fit my personal opinions. I don't believe that the Authorized King James Version is better than any other version of the Bible, but on the subject of Genesis, the Authorized King James Version works best for me.

For the sake of clarity and emphasis, throughout the book I have italicized certain words in some of the Bible verses that were not normally italicized. These changes have been noted in brackets beneath the verse.

Part I

Opening Your Mind to the
Genesis Story of Creation

Bridging the Gulf

God's spoken Word created universal spiritual laws that created the laws of physics and the laws for life forms. The universe and all living things are the results of these universal spiritual laws.

Following the process of God's spoken Word of creation, we shall see how the days of creation created the laws of physics and the spiritual laws of life forms.

Then, we will explore the process of evolution and the spiritual laws governing life. As a natural outcome of this discussion, the reader should come to an amazing understanding. If the Bible is understood correctly, there is no conflict with the written Word of God and scientific evidence.

We can let the Scriptures interpret the Scriptures, as God instructed us to do, or we can continue to apply our worldly understanding to the Bible and make God's Word look foolish. Scientists have looked long and hard in their search for truth concerning our physical universe. If Christians are to know the truth concerning both the spiritual universe and the physical universe, they must also search long and hard. No longer can believers simply read Bible verses and apply their own understanding to God's Word.

What does the Bible say about creation?

It is written that God created the heavens, the earth, and living things (including man) in six days. On the seventh day, He rested.

When God wanted to create anything, He would speak words, and His Creation would be manifested.

The Bible does not say how long creation days were. If creation days were only twenty-four hours long, evolution would have been impossible. On the other hand, if creation days were longer periods of time, God could have used evolution as a tool in creation.

Many Christians believe the days of creation were periods of time. Others believe the days of creation were only twenty-four hours long.

What does science say about evolution and the origins of our universe?

Scientists believe that about 3.8 billion years ago, all life evolved from simple bacteria from a single origin (Mayr 2001).

Evolution is a complex subject, but for our purpose a simple explanation will suffice. In the process of evolving, parents produce more offspring than is necessary to ensure survival of their species. By chance, some of their offspring are formed with different characteristics than their parents. If the new characteristics give the offspring a better chance of survival, they will pass these characteristics on to their young.

Scientists also commonly believe all space, time, and matter came into existence as the result of an incredibly large explosion around fifteen billion years ago (Asimov 1984). As matter cooled, the laws of physics came into being. The universe we know today was created as the cooling matter obeyed the laws of physics.

Could the creation story of the Bible and scientific explanations of evolution be one in the same?

Science is the study of nature, and nature is the result of God's spoken words; therefore, science is the study of God's manifested words.

Why does there seem to be such an incredible difference between the two explanations?

The confusion lies in our understanding of the written Word of God. Readers of the Bible apply their own understanding instead of searching the Scriptures to find God's intended meaning.

For instance, take the word "day." In the minds of most readers, the word "day" means one rotation of the planet Earth, which takes twenty-four hours to complete. After searching the Scriptures, some readers understand that in the Bible the word "day" can represent a period of time other than one rotation of the planet Earth. An example of a period of time being represented as a "day" is the forty years Israel spent in the desert.

> Harden not your heart, as in the provocation, *and* as *in* the day of temptation in the wilderness:
> When your fathers tempted me, proved me, and saw my work.
> Forty years long was I grieved with *this* generation, and said, It *is* a people that do err in their heart, and they have not known my ways:
> Psalms 95:8-10

Israel's day of temptation in the wilderness lasted for forty years. Another "day" in the Bible represents the law of God and has absolutely nothing to do with time.

> For the day of the Lord *is* near upon all the heathen: as thou hast done, it shall be done unto thee: thy reward shall return upon thine own head.
> Obadiah 1:15

The word "day" in this Bible verse represents God's karma-like law. Obviously, this day could not be twenty-four hours long.

Reconciling the biblical story of Genesis with scientific evidence is virtually impossible without first understanding exactly what a creation day is. We also need to have a deeper scriptural understanding of other words such as light, darkness, waters, firmament, divided waters, gathered waters, and dry *land*.

The key that will unlock true understanding of creation and reconcile biblical Genesis with scientific evidence is in obtaining new meanings for these words.

God's spoken Word, plus the substance of faith, created spiritual laws. These spiritual laws created the laws of physics. Our universe, and everything within it, was created with the laws of physics.

Scientists are correct when they say that creation was the result of physical laws. These physical laws, however, answer to higher spiritual laws.

The two explanations, as you will soon see, are complimentary.

Why is the scientific view of our origin so different from what is written in Genesis?

The problem is not with scientific understanding, nor the written Word of God. The problem is in our interpretation of the Bible. If the written Word is understood correctly, it is in line with scientific evidence but not necessarily with scientific theories. Scientific evidence is information that has been observed, classified, and verified by scientific methods to be accurate. Scientific theories are speculations about sets of facts and their relationships to each other.

To come to a deeper understanding of Genesis, we should use the Scriptures to interpret the Scriptures. It is written:

> For precept *must be* upon precept, precept upon precept;
> line upon line, line upon line; here a little, *and* there a little:
> Isaiah 28:10

When you read Genesis and see words like light, waters, firmament, and gathered waters, you should not add your worldly understanding to these words even if you get them from a Greek or Hebrew dictionary. A dictionary can be useful, but search the Scriptures for the scriptural meaning of these words. Many words in the Bible are given meanings you won't find in any dictionary.

Failure to let the Scriptures interpret the Scriptures will make the Book of Genesis sound like a fairytale, or magic.

Is there another source of information Christians are required by God to search?

Because that which may be known of God is manifest in them; for God hath shewed *it* unto them.

For the invisible things of him from the creation of the world are clearly seen, being understood by the things that are made, *even* his eternal power and Godhead; so that they are without excuse:

Romans 1:19-20

In simple terms, in these verses God is letting us know that if we study the things already made, or nature, He will manifest or reveal understanding about His internal power and Godhead.

God requires us to study what He has made. Science is the study of nature or manifested things. Scientific theories belong to scientists, but scientific facts belong to God. There is no difference in truthfulness between Bible facts and scientific evidence. If your understanding of the Bible doesn't line up with scientific evidence, you need to consider reevaluating your position.

Can Romans 1:19-20 be turned upside down?

If Romans 1:19-20 is true and we can know God by studying nature, then the opposite must be true also. By studying the Word of God, one can get a better understanding of nature. Science is the study of nature.

Wouldn't this be similar to looking at the sand in either the top or the bottom of an hourglass and deciding how much sand was in the opposite half? Maybe a farming analogy would be better than an hourglass analogy.

A farmer can make a good estimate as to the amount of harvest he might receive by looking at the amount of seed he will be planting. That same farmer could look at another farmer's harvest and come up with a good estimate of the amount of seed that was planted to produce the other farmer's harvest.

God's words were the seeds that created the world. It only makes sense that by looking at the world or things already made that one should be able to deduce important information concerning the seed (God's Word) and the farmer (God). The opposite should also be true. By studying God and His Word, one should be able to deduce information about things that are already made, or science.

If the preceding were not true, the case for being a God and the truthfulness of His written Word (the Bible) would become much weaker.

How long were creation days?

Thus the heavens and the earth were finished, and all the host of them.

And on the seventh day God ended his work which he had made; and he rested on the seventh day from all his work which he had made.

Genesis 2:1-2

There have always been questions in the minds of Bible readers. How did God create? Was there preexisting material? How long were the days of creation?

A small number of Christian fundamentalists believe creation days were twenty-four hours long. They also believe the universe is about ten thousand years old.

These believers often look to Exodus as proof.

For *in* six days the Lord made heaven and earth, the sea, and all that in them *is*, and rested the seventh day: wherefore the Lord blessed the sabbath day, and hallowed it.

Exodus 20:11

Italicized words in the Bible were not part of the original text; they were added for the sake of clarity. It is my opinion that in the above Bible verse the word "with" would have been a more appropriate word to add than the word "in."

In the more popular day-age theory, a creation day represents a longer period of time. This theory allows for a universe that is billions of years old. Millions of Christians share this belief.

Support for this idea that creation days were large periods of time with major events happening in them can be found throughout the Bible.

These *are* the generations of the heavens and of the earth when they were created, in the *day* that the Lord God made the earth and the heavens,

Genesis 2:4
[*second emphasis* added]

Some years ago in Oregon after visiting the John Day fossil beds, I overheard a conversation between two girls who could have been sisters. As they were walking to their car, the younger girl had a confused look on her face and said to the older girl, "I thought God created everything in six days. How could those bones be so old?" The older girl explained to her "The Bible does not say how long a day was when God created the world. A day back then could have been millions of years long." Her answer seemed to satisfy the younger girl.

God's creation days were not millions or billions of years old. Bible believers created this idea because twenty-four hour creation days did not agree with scientific evidence.

Could God have created everything in six, twenty-four hour days? Yes! Anything is possible with God (Luke 1:37).[1] Did God create everything in six, twenty-four hour days? Not according to scientific evidence.

Who is right? Who is wrong? I am proposing that both sides are wrong. Creation days have absolutely nothing to do with time.

Before I say what I believe a creation day is, allow me to tell you a sad but true story from my youth.

One day I was walking to Bible study class in Creston Elementary School in Creston, Ohio. I remember thinking the thought "It is written in the Bible that God created everything in just six days. That's ridiculous, how can anyone believe that way? How can I believe anything that is written in the Bible?"

How many others used this same excuse for not following God's written Word?

What was the true nature of a creation day?

A creation day was not a twenty-four hour period nor was it a large period of time in which God created something. The days of creation had nothing to do with time and everything to do with creative Word from God.

Word from God manifested into things like light, firmament, gathered waters, dry *land*, and lights in the firmament of heaven. These manifested words were the days of creation. For example, Day One was "light," not the time it took to create light.

Each day of creation had an evening and then a morning. Evenings and mornings were not times within days; they were manifestations of God's spoken Word. In the case of Day One, darkness was the evening, and light was the morning of the first day. As manifested Word of God, the days of creation were the source of all physical laws in the universe. There will be more on this subject later in this book.

Have you ever considered that the days of creation could have been something other than periods of time? As we proceed through the days of creation, keep an open mind. After seeing the evidence, there will be plenty of time to make up your mind one way or another.

Are there patterns within creation days?

Each creation day was created with three sets of "Let there be" statements from God. This is a major piece of the puzzle concerning the biblical story of creation.

As with every puzzle, one has to find the correct pieces and place them in the correct places. In some instances, the "Let there be" statement was hidden (not spoken). In other instances, it was spoken but found within another day.

The good news is that the puzzle has already been put together. All we need to do is to take it apart, one piece at a time, and examine each piece, or "Let there be" statement.

The main thing to remember is that all creation days, sooner or later, have three "Let there be" statements from God. This pattern is repeated throughout the Bible. Whenever God wanted to create a new day or law, He would speak three sets of creative words, which manifested an evening, a morning, and a seed in the form of light.

Jesus also used this pattern of three when He wanted Peter to head His church on earth. Jesus said to Peter, "Feed my lamb, feed my sheep, and feed my sheep" (John 21:15-17).[2]

When Jesus wanted the gospel to be preached to the Gentiles, He showed Peter in a vision all manners of four-footed beasts of the earth, wild beasts, creeping things, and fowls of the air and told him three times to rise, kill, and eat (Acts 10:11-16).[3]

In a later chapter called "Bible Mysteries," we will see that even the number of the antichrist's name, which is 666, lends creditability to the hypothesis that it takes three "Let there be" statements to make a day.

Why would it take three "Let there be" statements to create a single day? I believe it has to do with the Holy Trinity. God is three persons but only one God. Or maybe it has to do with dimensions, or both.

The making of a new day or kingdom is a fascinating subject, which we will return to at a later time.

How did I know there were three "Let there be" statements for each day of creation?

There are patterns everywhere in nature. Nature repeats itself over and over. The yearly growth rings of a tree, cell creation, and blades of grass are examples of things that can be found everywhere in nature. Nature is the manifested Word of God; therefore, God is responsible for the patterns we find in nature.

I noticed in Genesis that creation days three, four, and six all had three sets of "Let there be" statements. Knowing that God is a God of order and knowing His fondness for the use of patterns, I wondered why all of the creation days didn't have three "Let there be" statements within them.

After much searching, thought, and prayer I came to the realization that there are always three "Let there be" statements for each creation day even if they can't be seen. Also, if a "Let there be" statement could not be easily seen for a certain day, there was always a good reason for it to be missing or hidden. As you will see in the following pages, hidden "Let there be" statements are extremely important clues to how God made His creation. (See Appendix A)

Was light the first thing created?

Remember that each day of creation had an evening and then a morning. Evenings and mornings were not times within days. They were manifestations of the Word of God, or created things.

> And the earth was without form, and void; and *darkness was* upon the face of the deep. And the Spirit of God moved upon the face of the *waters.*
>
> Genesis 1:2
> [*emphasis* added]

Note that darkness and waters were already present in the second verse of the first chapter of Genesis, indicating that they both had already been created. We know the Word of God and the substance of faith were the recipe for the creation of both the darkness and the waters because we can see this in Hebrews 11:1-3 and John 1:3. Since they were created before God made the physical universe, both the darkness and the waters must have been nonphysical in nature.

The darkness mentioned in Genesis 1:2 could not have been lack of light as we commonly understand it to be. In Genesis 1:4, God divided the light from the darkness after light had been created. If darkness was just the lack of light, there could not have been any darkness after the light was created.

Understanding that darkness was something other than the lack of light did not come easily to me. Bible verses of Isaiah 45:7, Matthew 6:23, and Matthew 8:12 helped me see the light, or in this case the darkness.

> I form the light, and create darkness: I make peace, and create evil: I the Lord do all these *things*.
>
> Isaiah 45:7

> But if thine eye be evil, thy whole body shall be full of darkness. If therefore the light that is in thee be darkness, how great *is* that darkness!
>
> Matthew 6:23

> But the children of the kingdom shall be cast out into outer darkness: there shall be weeping and gnashing of teeth.
>
> Matthew 8:12

Surely the outer darkness in Matthew 8:12 must be some kind of substance, or some kind of light.

The evening of Day One was a created thing called darkness. It was *not* actually written, "Let there be darkness," but in Isaiah 45:7 God said He had created darkness.

Why were the words "Let there be darkness" and "Let there be waters" not actually written in the Book of Genesis when God must have spoken them? Maybe this universe was not God's first attempt (Rothaman 1995). There is no way to know if other universes preceded our universe or not, but God is perfect, and practice makes perfect.

If there was an earlier universe, the waters present on Day One could have been the residue from that universe. It might be that darkness was a spiritual substance from spiritual heavens that was destroyed in the previous universe.

Maybe the words God spoke to create the darkness and the waters were spoken within the previous universe before the end of its time. Maybe the spoken Word that created the darkness and the waters caused the end of the previous universe. There have been some who have suggested that our current universe is just one in a long line of universes (Ronan 1993).

Faith

Some say faith is belief in something. Some say it is acting upon what is believed. One of the definitions written in *Merriam Webster's Collegiate Dictionary,* 10th Edition, is "belief and trust in and loyalty to God."

Now faith is the *substance* of things hoped for, the evidence of things not seen.
Through faith we understand that the worlds were framed by the word of God, so that things which are seen were not made of things which do appear.

Hebrews 11:1,3
[emphasis added]

As we can see from these two Bible verses, faith is a substance. Does the word "substance" seem to be out of place when describing faith?

Faith is an invisible spiritual matter, something to be felt or believed. Substance on the other hand seems to be something one might expect to experience here in the physical world. But yet, we know the word "substance" can also be used to describe objects and situations.

I am going to present a new idea or concept that might at first seem to be out of place, but give it time. Think about it. Like the word "substance" in Hebrews 11:1, you might end up liking it.

There is another aspect to faith. I believe faith was and is previously manifested Word of God, which has accomplished its assignment and been released to return unto God. Word returning to God is only possible if it has been judged to have completed its work.

So shall my word be that goeth forth out of my mouth: *it shall not return unto me void*, but it shall accomplish that which I please, and it shall prosper *in the thing* whereto I sent it.

Isaiah 55:11
[*first emphasis* added]

Romans 10:17 tells us that faith comes by hearing, and hearing by the Word of God. Why couldn't the Word of God we receive, believe, and obey be judged by God to become faith? After all, the Word of God is a spiritual substance.

If faith is previously manifested Word of God that was judged to have finished its assigned task, whom or what does the judging? I believe it is name from God that does the judging of previously manifested Word. The names of Day, Night, Heaven, Earth, and Seas were given to light, darkness, firmament, dry *land*, and gathered waters in order to judge previously manifested Word of God. Within each name there are sets of three "Let there be" statements from God. Faith combines with the Word of God, or "Let there be" statements, to form God's creations.

How can we know there are three "Let there be" statements in the names from God such as Day, Night, Heaven, Earth, and Seas? That's a fair question.

We know it takes three "Let there be" statements to make a creation day. If I haven't given you enough evidence to prove this yet, just keep an open mind. Much more evidence lies ahead in this book.

Now, as for knowing that there are three "Let there be" statements in names from God, this takes a leap of faith. Readers must decide for themselves if they are willing to make the leap or not. I encourage you to do so. You can always jump back if you don't like what you see over here.

How does faith work in the modern world?

Believing and obeying Jesus is the manifestation or completion of God's Word. The name of Jesus releases completed words to be formed into faith substance. If the faith substance is judged worthy, the promises in the name of Jesus are received. Jesus is the author and finisher of our faith.

Looking unto Jesus the author and finisher of *our* faith; who for the joy that was set before him endured the cross, despising the shame, and is set down at the right hand of the throne of God.

Hebrews 12:2

It doesn't matter whether it is the Old Testament or the New Testament; the pattern is the same. Receiving of name from God is first, obeying and forming faith are second, trials and temptations come next, and finally, there is receiving the promises within the name.

God gave mankind the task of choosing whether to believe, trust, or obey the Word of God. What about inanimate objects? Do things have the choice to obey God?

Humans choose to use faith, and God judges their faith in order to bring forth promises or works found in the written Word of God. In the case of inanimate objects, I believe their faith is released as the result of becoming what God's Word commands them to become. An example of this would be when God told the waters under firmament to be gathered unto one place, and they obeyed. As the result of their obeying God and becoming gathered waters, faith was released. God used this very faith and His words "Let the dry *land* appear" to form some of the gathered waters into dry *land*.

Until I started my search for the truth about Genesis, I had never thought about inanimate objects having faith, except for maybe mustard seeds (Matthew 17:20)[4] and the Word of God. This brings us

31

back to a familiar point. One must be willing to set aside old beliefs in order to obtain deeper understandings.

Is everything Word?

God created everything with His spoken Word and faith. God's words are the image of His will with the power to bring about His will. God's will is law; therefore, God's words are law and power.

Scientists tell us that everything is created out of energy that obeys the laws of physics, which are within energy. Laws of physics within energy and word with power mean the same thing. There is no difference between what is written in the Bible and scientific facts when both are understood correctly.

If you were to hold a baby in your arms, know that you are holding energy that obeys the laws of physics and that you are holding the manifested Word of God.

Part II

Creation Days One Through Six

Day One

The Substance of Light

In the beginning God created the heaven and the earth.

And the earth was without form, and void; and darkness *was* upon the face of the deep. And the Spirit of God moved upon the face of the waters.

And God said, Let there be light: and there was light.

And God saw the light, that *it was* good: and God divided the light from the darkness.

And God called the light Day, and the darkness he called Night. And the evening and the morning were the first day.

Genesis 1:1-5

As you read the words written in the Bible concerning creation, please keep the following in mind. God spoke these written words at one time to a prophet who gave them to God's people. The words He spoke to the prophet are not actually the words God used to form all of creation. They only represent the words God used to create everything He made.

You may ask what the difference is. The difference is that one set of words from God was used to create and the other set of words from God was used to give understanding to man concerning how God created. Knowing there is a difference between the words God spoke to create and the words He spoke to inform will help facilitate your understanding concerning creation.

God first formed the laws of creation in His mind and in His heart. After all, man was made in God's image and likeness and like God we create images in our minds and hearts before creating anything.

How did God create light?

God used Word and substance of faith to manifest the images that were in His mind and heart into the laws of creation.

Now faith is the substance of things hoped for, the evidence of things not seen.
For by it the elders obtained a good report.
Through faith we understand that the worlds were framed by the word of God, so that things which are seen were not made of things which do appear.

Hebrews 11:1-3

God gave birth to His spoken Word, which carried out His will. Within God's Word was the instruction and power to accomplish all God desired. Nothing was created without God's Word (John 1:3).[5]

Was light something other than sunlight?

Until I began my search for truth concerning the origins of the universe, I don't remember ever entertaining the thought that the light God created on Day One could have been something other than the electromagnetic energy we receive from our sun. However, that is exactly what I am asking you to consider. Resist the urge to apply your mind's understanding of light, and let the Scriptures interpret the Scriptures.

There are other examples of light in the Bible, such as this verse about spiritual light:

Giving thanks unto the Father, which hath made us meet
to be partakers of the inheritance of the saints in light:

Colossians 1:12

As well, we see in the First Book of Timothy where Jesus dwells
in a light no man can approach or see.

Who only hath immortality, dwelling in the light which
no man can approach unto; whom no man hath seen, nor can
see: to whom *be* honour and power everlasting. Amen.

I Timothy 6:16

Paul tells us of the time when Jesus spoke to him, and a light from
heaven shined with a brightness above the sun. No doubt, Paul was
speaking of some kind of spiritual light.

At mid-day, O king, I saw in the way a light from heaven,
above the brightness of the sun, shining round about me and
them which journeyed with me.

Acts 26:13

The Bible is full of nonphysical light. In the First Book of John we
see that God is a type of light.

This then is the message which we have heard of him, and
declare unto you, that God is light, and in him is no darkness
at all.

I John 1:5

Considering the preceding Bible verses, the light of Day One
could have easily been something other than physical in nature.
Since suns or stars were not created until Day Four, the likelihood of
Day One's light being something other than the light of this world is
all but certain.

It only makes sense that Day One's light was a higher energy substance than the light of this world, or electromagnetic energy (Jones 1992). God rules the heavens, and the heavens rule the earth, or all physical matter. The light created on Day One was the spiritual energy substance that God used to create the spiritual world of light, or the Kingdom of Light.

If Day One's light was not the same as the light of our world, why did God call it light?

If you wanted to describe the ocean to primitive people who never saw an ocean, it would be a good idea to start your conversation by calling a local lake a very, very, very small ocean. In giving the name of "light" to what was created on the first day, God was just giving us a clue to its true nature.

What do we know about light?

With help from the written Word, there are some things we know concerning the light of Day One. It was created in the midst of the darkness that was present before God started to speak the words that would bring forth His Creation. After being created, light was removed from the darkness.

We also know that light was created with the Word of God and the substance of faith. Since the Word of God is spiritual law and faith is a substance, the light of Day One was a spiritual law substance. God's spoken Word is God's will. Spiritual law substance is the image of God's will. Each creation day is the image of God's will, not a period of time.

I imagine an image of God's will is like a vision with substance that has the power and authority to make images within other less powerful substances.

How did God create images of His will?

God's words are God's will and are spiritual law. Faith is God's previously spoken Word that was judged to have completed its assigned task. Faith belongs to whomever or whatever obeyed God's spoken Word to allow God's spoken words to complete their task.

God's words "Let there be darkness" created darkness. These same words were released as faith once the darkness had been created and the words were judged to have completed their assigned task. God's spoken words "Let there be light" and His previously spoken words "Let there be darkness," which had become faith, created the light of Day One.

I knew for years that creation days were spiritual law substances because the Word of God and the substance of faith created them. Then one day I read in the eighth chapter of Ezekiel where God took Ezekiel to a place that was between the earth and the heaven. The place where God took Ezekiel was an image of Jerusalem and the temple. In this place Ezekiel was shown that in order for God to punish certain people in the earth for doing evil, He had them punished in this spiritual place first. That led me to two understandings.

The first one was that creation days, which are spiritual law substances, are actually the images of God's will. Secondly, I realized I needed to create good images in my spiritual heart because good images led to good things happening here in the earth, and bad images led to bad things happening here in the earth.

Did each day have both an evening and a morning?

The morning portion of the first day was light. Light was removed from the darkness, or evening part of the first day.

Every day had an evening and a morning, even if it was not written in the form of a "Let there be" statement. For example, in Day One, "Let there be darkness" was not written, but we know darkness was there. According to Isaiah 45:7, that darkness was a created thing. We also know that darkness can be a type of light.

But if thine eye be evil, thy whole body shall be full of darkness. If therefore the *light* that is in thee be *darkness*, how great *is* that darkness!

Matthew 6:23

[*first two emphases* added]

What was the last thing created in each day?

Eventually, every day also produced more than an evening and a morning. It would also issue seed in the form of light from that particular day, which I shall refer to as seed light. In the case of the first day, God divided the light from the darkness. The seed light of each day was always divided from the day in which it was created. This is a major key or clue to understanding Genesis.

Each day of creation reveals secrets that are hidden in the other days of creation. When I found a clue in any one of the creation days, I would then try to apply it to the rest of the creation days.

Seed light from creation days has a lot in common with the seed of this world. Seed allows new plants to become images of their parent plants. The same law that created the older plants also created the new plants. Seed light uses the same three "Let there be" statements, which created the day it was issued from to create images of that day elsewhere.

Seed light also forms images of their parent days by passing along the law of their parents; therefore, seed light can be considered to be the seed of creation days.

Why were evenings and mornings opposites?

Every creation day had an evening and then a morning. Evening and morning are two parts of one thing, a day. I want you to notice that they are opposites. Darkness was the evening of Day One, and light was the morning of Day One. Can any two things be more different than darkness and light? Yet, together they are one thing, which was the first day.

Day Two

The Substance of Firmament

> And God said, Let there be a firmament in the midst of the waters, and let it divide the waters from the waters.
>
> And God made the firmament, and divided the waters which *were* under the firmament from the waters which *were* above the firmament: and it was so.
>
> And God called the firmament Heaven. And the evening and the morning were the second day.
>
> Genesis 1:6-8

What was firmament?

The Hebrew and Chaldee Dictionary in the back of my Authorized King James Version of the Bible defines the word "firmament" as being an expanse. The dictionary (Merriam Webster 1993) has two definitions for the word "expanse." The first definition is "firmament," and the second one is "great extent of something spread out."

One can easily picture an expanse as an ocean on a calm day, an open prairie, or a flat desert. Even a spilled bucket of water on a flat surface could suffice as an expanse.

Every day had an evening and a morning within them, and eventually, a seed light was divided from each day. Since firmament was created in the midst of the waters in the same manner as light was created in the darkness, the waters were the evening part of the second day since darkness was the evening part of the first day.

What were the waters?

Firmament formed in the midst of the waters. The waters of our universe were created sometime after our universe was born. The waters that were present when God spoke the words, "Let there be light," could not have been H_2O. Prelight waters were an energy substance that the Word of God and the substance of faith used to form prephysical energy and then physical energy. In the Bible, water is sometimes referred to as spirit (John 4:13-14)[6] and sometimes as people (Revelation 17:15),[7] so it isn't surprising that water could be something besides H_2O. I believe the waters were the evening part of the second day of creation, and they could have been residue from a previous universe.

What was the nature of firmament?

Firmament also has different meanings. The firmament we are considering caused the waters to divide; that is, it gave law in the form of force to the waters. Therefore, firmament was probably a spiritual substance that released its energy to give law or force to the prephysical world.

God called the firmament Heaven. There is both a physical heaven with stars and other planets like the one we live in and spiritual heavens with spiritual beings.

Since light was a spiritual law substance that was probably placed within the Spirit of God, and physical suns and planets were not yet created, it would be reasonable to believe that firmament was also a spiritual law substance where God placed the spiritual heaven. Firmament, the morning of Day Two, must have been a type of spiritual space and energy.

What does it mean that firmament was a type of spiritual space and energy?

When we think about space in this universe, we think of a place where physical objects like suns, planets, moon, comets, and meteorites can end up. If one of these objects ends up in a part of space, gravity will also be there.

Firmament is the space where spiritual objects may be found. If a spiritual object does end up in the space that is firmament, there would also be spiritual energy there.

Were the waters opposite of firmament?

Let's take one more look at my theory of opposites. On Day One, the evening (darkness) was the opposite of the morning (light). Maybe all evenings are the opposites of all mornings. If so, the evening of Day Two (waters) would have been the opposite of the morning of Day Two (firmament).

Day Three

The Substance of Dry *Land*

And God said, Let the waters under the heaven be gathered together unto one place, and let the dry *land* appear: and it was so.

And God called the dry *land* Earth; and the gathering together of the waters called he Seas: and God saw that *it was* good.

Genesis 1:9-10

What was created on Day Three?

According to my hypothesis, the days of creation were spiritual law substances, or images of God's will, which were the source for the fundamental forces of our physical universe. Fundamental forces created our universe and our planet Earth. Think of the third day as the creation of our universe, not just our planet.

The laws of physics obeyed on our planet are also obeyed everywhere in the universe.

If I were to go outside, pick up a handful of soil, and then examine each atom, no atom would be unique to the planet Earth. Atoms consist of at least one electron and one proton, which are held together with electromagnetic force. They exist alone or in combinations and are building blocks of everything that we see (Jones 1992).

Scientists say it is a fact that our planet and our bodies are made of elements formed within suns that went supernova (explosion of a large star) (Gribbin 1999). God's Word cannot disagree with scientific facts, for they are both God's laws. With this statement in mind, Day Three must be about the creation of the physical universe, not just the planet Earth.

If the planet Earth was the only planet to be created when God said, "Let dry *land* appear," when did he create all the other planets and non-star heavenly bodies? Did He speak one planet at a time into existence? Why didn't God mention when He created them? Surely when He spoke dry *land* into existence, He created what would become our universe, not just our planet.

Were the waters an energy substance?

As previously stated, the waters were present before God spoke on Day One. Chances are good that the waters were residue from a previous universe. In any case, they could not have been H_2O. Scientists know that the waters (H_2O) of this physical universe did not manifest until some time after the universe started to form. Whatever the waters were, God used them to create both the heavenly universe and the physical universe.

God's spoken words, "Let the waters under heaven be gathered " along with the waters under firmament, manifested into a substance called gathered waters. Gathered waters were the evening of the third day of creation. Gathered waters became the cosmic egg from which our physical universe was hatched.

According to my hypothesis, evenings and mornings were opposites. Since the evening of Day Three was gathered waters, the morning of Day Three would be scattered gathered waters (dry *land*).

God said, "Let the dry *land* appear," and caused the substance of gathered waters to manifest into dry *land*, the morning of the third day. It happened with a bang—a big bang—as described by scientists. The gathered waters exploded into the curved space dimension that we call our universe. Gathered waters became scattered gathered waters, or dry *land*. Dry *land* (physical matter of our universe) has two forms, mass matter and nonmass matter (waters). Nonmass matter (waters) are nonmass particle-energy fields such as gravitons and neutrinos.

What do scientists say about the big-bang theory?

Galaxies are moving away from each other. By reversing the motion of their expansion, scientists can estimate the time when our universe exploded into existence. They believe the big bang occurred less than twenty billion years ago but more than nine billion years ago. Fifteen billion years ago seems to be a reasonable estimate for the beginning of time.

Scientists don't know if the big bang was preceded by a big crunch (the compression of a previous universe) or just popped out of nothing (Rothaman 1995). I hypothesis that there was a previous universe, and after this universe ends another will follow.

This universe will end in the same manner as the last universe ended. God will speak the three "Let there be" statements that were not written in the first chapter of the Book of Genesis. These are "Let the light be divided from the darkness," which will place all that belongs to God, within God; "Let there be darkness," which will dissolve all spiritual matter into spiritual energy; and "Let there be waters," which will dissolve all matter into energy.

In the universe that will follow the universe we live in, some confused fellow will wonder for years why these three "Let there be" statements were not written when God must have spoken them.

What was dry *land*?

Gathered waters and dry *land* were not two separate things; they were two parts of one thing, which was Day Three. The two forces that created gathered waters and dry *land* were really only one force, which was the strong force.

Strong nuclear force operates only within the nucleus of atoms, which it holds together. A nucleus consists of protons and neutrons. Protons are positively charged with electromagnetic energy.

Neutrons are really only protons that are neutral; that is, they don't feel the electromagnetic force. Protons repulse each other with tremendous force. It's the strong nuclear force that holds nucleus (protons and neutrons) together. On a darker note, it is strong nuclear force that releases the power of atomic bombs (Jones 1992).

How did electromagnetic force come to be?

And God said, Let the earth bring forth grass, the herb yielding seed, *and* the fruit tree yielding fruit after his kind, whose seed *is* in itself, upon the earth: and it was so.

And the earth brought forth grass, *and* herb yielding seed after his kind, and the tree yielding fruit, whose seed *was* in itself, after his kind: and God saw that *it was* good.

And the evening and the morning were the third day.

Genesis 1:11-13

When God spoke those words to the earth (dry *land*, or our physical universe), dry *land* exploded or decayed into particles with electric charges to create the electromagnetic force (Jones 1992). The electromagnetic force is the fundamental physical force responsible for the emission and absorption of photons and for interactions between charged particles.

Electrons and nuclei (protons and neutrons) are held together to form atoms by the electromagnetic force (Coulomb force). In nature, atoms can be found in about ninety elements combined to make compounds, and compounds combined to create mixtures.

Were grass, herbs, and trees the same as electromagnetic force?

Since plants are formed from elements, compounds, and mixtures and they live on electromagnetic energy (light), there simply could not be any grass, herbs, or trees without the electromagnetic force. After God created the plants, He said that it was good. What could He have meant by that? Since God judges man's spirit and heart, which gives law to man, wouldn't God have been looking at the laws that were responsible for grass, herbs, and trees? Surely the electromagnetic force is a residue of the force that caused dry *land* or mass matter to appear.

Where does the force of gravity come from?

Before dry *land* appeared, God spoke the words "Let the waters under heaven be gathered together." These words caused the waters under heaven to be attracted to itself, which caused the waters to become concentrated.

God's spoken words, "Let dry *land* appear," caused gathered waters to transform into energy matter of our universe. Gravity or curved space is a residue affect of the force, which gathered the waters together. The force of gravity is trying to return dry *land* back into its original state of being gathered waters.

Why is there a struggle between mornings and evenings?

Light (morning of Day One) was opposite of darkness (evening of Day One). Firmament (morning of Day Two) was opposite of waters (evening of Day Two). It is only reasonable to believe that dry *land* (morning of Day Three) was opposite of gathered waters (evening of Day Three).

Mornings and evenings are engaged in struggles that will not stop until our universe ceases to exist. It is this struggle that gave each creation day the ability to do its work.

In a way, it is like the relationship between men and women who are made opposite of each other so they can have children. Mornings and evenings were also made opposite of each other so they could produce seed light to produce images of themselves.

Can we share the name Earth?

Before moving on, we need to emphasize a very important point about Day Three. When God gave the name Earth to dry *land*, He was naming all physical energy (matter and nonmatter), not just our planet. As long as one is locked into the belief that the name Earth belongs only to our planet, Genesis will always be a mystery to that person.

A long time ago, man gave up the belief that the Earth was the center of the universe and that all the heavenly bodies rotated around it. Today, for the sake of increasing our knowledge, we must share the name Earth with the entire universe, or all physical matter.

What's in a name?

We need to return to the subject of name. Why did God call light, Day; darkness, Night; dry *land*, Earth; and gathered waters, Seas? What purpose did this giving of names serve? Remember, at that time there were no people. It is written that when God does a new thing, He first tells what He is going to do.

> Behold, the former things are come to pass, and new things do I declare: before they spring forth I tell you of them.
>
> Isaiah 42:9

Could the giving of name by God have been an announcement of what He was about to do? Maybe the name given by God prepared the way for the coming of a promised thing from God. Maybe the promises of God are within the name given.

Name from God was Word from God. As seen in the following Bible verse, Word of God and the substance of faith were used by God to create the worlds.

Through faith we understand that the worlds were *framed by the word of God*, so that things which are seen were not made of things which do appear.

Hebrews 11:3

[*emphasis* added]

Whenever God wanted to create a new thing, He spoke words, or names.

Name from God gives the receiver of the name the ability to give faith back to God. Faith is needed to receive the promises of God. For example, the name Heaven gave firmament the ability to give faith back to God. Faith from firmament was used to bring forth promises of God within the name Heaven. The three "Let there be lights," which God spoke on the fourth day, were the promises within the name Heaven.

The names Day, Night, Earth, and Seas caused light, darkness, dry *land*, and gathered waters to manifest days seven, three, six, and five. Days one and two were created after God named the void and the face of the waters with Spirits of God. (See Appendix B)

Were the void and the waters given names?

Allow me to explain why I believe that both void and the waters were each given a Spirit of God for their name. Names are words from God; therefore, they are spirits from God. God's Word is spirit and life (John 6:63).[8]

It is written that there are seven Spirits of God that go to all the earth (Revelation 5:6).[9] If there were less than seven name spirits, I would be wondering why.

Remember how dry *land* was created and given the name Earth before gathered waters received the name Seas even though gathered waters was created first? Also, remember how light was created and given the name Day before darkness received the name Night even though darkness was created first? There is a pattern here. After

50

*HOW GOD USED BOTH HIS SPOKEN WORD
AND EVOLUTION TO CREATE MAN*

considering this pattern and the need for seven name spirits, adding another Spirit of God to the puzzle was a logical choice.

When did the Spirit of God arrive?

I would like to address a question that puzzled me for many years.

Wasn't darkness already created before the Spirit of God arrived upon the face of the waters? If so, how could darkness be the evening of the first day? My puzzlement started and finished with the word "moved." Moved did not mean arrived, it meant to flutter or to shake. The Bible does not say when the Spirit of God arrived at the scene. As far as I can see, the two Spirits of God, who were not mentioned by name, could have been spoken within a previous creation. They could have caused the end of a previous creation.

> And the earth was without form, and void; and darkness *was* upon the face of the deep. And the spirit of God *moved* upon the face of the waters.
>
> Genesis 1:2
> [*second emphasis* added]

Are the creation days like trees?

Before you started to read this book, you probably thought the creation days were periods of time. I have presented the possibility that they were not periods of time at all but were created things. Each day had an evening, a morning, and eventually, each day released seed light.

Jesus often used analogies to describe difficult concepts. In order to understand "creation days" better, I also will use an analogy.

God's spoken words were like seeds. When God spoke the words "Let the waters under heaven be gathered together unto one place. .," His words went into the waters under firmament like seeds into the ground. God's spoken words and the waters under firmament manifested into the "gathered waters," which were the evening of the third day and the cosmic seed from which our universe came.

God's spoken words, "Let dry *land* appear" along with the gathered waters, manifested into our universe with a big bang.

To continue the analogy, the gathering of the waters or the evening of Day Three would be like the time when seeds developed roots in the darkness of the soil. Creation of dry *land,* or the morning of Day Three, would be like when a tree comes out of the darkness of the soil into the light of the day as part of the tree that is visible to our eyes.

The third "Let there be" statement of Day Three was the Word of God that caused dry *land* to bring forth grass, herbs, and trees, which I claim to be electromagnetic energy as seed light of the third day.

I have several reasons for believing that grass, herbs, and trees were really electromagnetic energy. First, scientists know that when our universe was very young, the strong nuclear particles deteriorated into particles with electromagnetic energy.

Secondly, there could be no grass, herbs, or trees without electromagnetic energy because it is responsible for elements, compounds, and mixtures.

Thirdly, I believe when God named His Creation grass, herbs, and trees instead of calling it an electromagnetic force, it was an extremely clever way for Him to hide the truth in His written Word until the time He wanted to reveal it.

Lastly, I could not explain how God created plants before He created the sun.

To understand my theory of creation days better, try thinking of the three "Let there be" statements spoken on Day Three in this manner. The first "Let there be" statement was the seed that created the evening of Day Three as root in the darkness of the soil. The second "Let there be" statement was the seed that created the morning of Day Three as the trunk of the tree that grew out of the darkness of the soil into the sunlight of the day. The last "Let there be" statement of Day Three was the seed that caused the tree to produce fruit and seed as seed light. Each day of creation can be thought of as working in a similar manner.

Day Four

The Kingdom of Lights

> And God said, Let there be lights in the firmament of the heaven to divide the day from the night; and let them be for signs, and for seasons, and for days, and years:
>
> And let them be for lights in the firmament of the heaven to give light upon the earth: and it was so.
>
> And God made two great lights; the greater light to rule the day, and the lesser light to rule the night: *he made* the stars also.
>
> And God set them in the firmament of the heaven to give light upon the earth,
>
> And to rule over the day and over the night, and to divide the light from the darkness: and God saw that *it was* good.
>
> And the evening and the morning were the fourth day.
>
> Genesis 1:14-19

Were the greater and lesser lights our sun and moon?

At first glance it would seem obvious that the greater light was our sun and the lesser light was our moon. Remember that we are to let the Scriptures interpret the Scriptures. Seek knowledge in the Bible, not what is already in your head.

In the Milky Way Galaxy there are a few hundred billion stars, and in the universe there are several hundred billion galaxies (Gribbin 1999). Our sun is a star and subject to the same laws of physics as every other star in the sky. Also, scientists say that our sun is a second or third generation star, not the first star ever made. We can see in Genesis 1:16 that God didn't make the stars (physical world stars) until after He had created both the greater and lesser lights.

It would be reasonable to believe that the lights of Day Four were made of spiritual law substance, which would later give the physical world the universal law of weak nuclear force. Weak nuclear force is the fundamental physical force responsible for particle decay processes. It also governs interactions between hadrons and leptons.

The important thing to understand about weak nuclear force and the decay process that it governs is the mechanism by which stars release their energy as light. The suns (stars) of this universe provide sunlight or electromagnetic energy, but it is the weak nuclear force (light from the lights in the firmament of heaven, Day Four) that gives light to our universe to create suns.

There could be no physical light upon the earth without the weak force. Our sun and all the stars in our universe are physical images of Day Four, which are lights in the firmament of heaven. The creation of the greater and lesser lights was most likely the evening part of Day Four. The morning portion of Day Four was created when God said, "Let them be for signs, and for seasons, and for days, and years." Then God's spoken words, "And let them be for lights in the firmament of the heaven to give light upon the earth," created the seed light of Day Four.

Please notice that the light of Day Four does not stay with Day Four. It was to give light upon the earth, which was Day Three of creation.

How does light reach the physical world?

If my hypothesis is correct, and the lights in the firmament of heaven are nonphysical in nature, just how does their light reach or affect our physical universe? Firmament was responsible for dividing the waters on Day Two; therefore, firmament was attached to or was part of the waters under firmament. The waters under firmament were gathered together and became the cosmic egg from which our universe was hatched. Therefore, our physical universe was attached to the heavenly universe, which was, in turn, attached to the spiritual law substance of lights in the firmament of heaven.

Are there two types of name from God?

Mankind uses their hands to accomplish their will. God uses spoken words to create. Like man, God has two types of hands. God's left-hand name, or word, created the first seven days of creation as impersonal spiritual law substances. God's right-hand name gave life to His Creation.

What is the difference between right-hand and left-hand name?

God didn't give name to the greater light nor the lesser light on Day Four. God waited until after the seventh day to give them names. Both the greater and lesser lights were to receive a different kind of name from God; they would receive right-hand name.

Left-hand name from God caused the receiver of left-hand name to develop a day that was complete with an evening, a morning, and a seed light from that day. Right-hand name from God, received after the seventh day, gave life to the receiver of right-hand name. Receiver of right-hand name would develop mind, soul, and heart.

Could there be spiritual universes?

Some people have problems with the possibility of there being other universes in other dimensions. Why is it so hard to believe that there could be other universes with energy matter different from the energy matter of our universe?

Could it be that people who have trouble imagining other worlds have not really thought about the world we live in? We really do live in an amazing universe.

If it were possible to go to the edge of our universe and shine a light all the way across it, it would take the light thirty billion light years to arrive on the other side. When one considers that light travels in a vacuum at about 186,281 miles per second, in thirty billion light years the light would have traveled one hundred and eighty sextillion miles (Jones 1992).

Anyone who meditates on these incredibly large numbers should find it easier to believe in the possibility of other spiritual worlds. As a matter of fact, I believe God guarantees it.

Because that which may be known of God is manifest in them; for God hath shewed *it* unto them.

For the invisible things of him from the creation of the world are clearly seen, being understood by the things that are made, *even* his eternal power and Godhead; so that they are without excuse:

Romans 1:19-20

Day Five

The Kingdom of Creatures

And God said, Let the waters bring forth abundantly the moving creature that hath life, and fowl *that* may fly above the earth in the open firmament of heaven.

And God created great whales, and every living creature that moveth, which the waters brought forth abundantly, after their kind, and every winged fowl after his kind: and God saw that *it was* good.

And God blessed them, saying, Be fruitful, and multiply, and fill the waters in the seas, and let fowl multiply in the earth.

And the evening and the morning were the fifth day.

Genesis 1:20-23

Is evolution a scientific fact?

I saw a television program on my local Public Broadcasting Station. Scientists are studying the genetic material of all life on earth starting with microscopic organisms found around ocean vents thousands of feet below the surface. Sunlight doesn't reach the depths of the vents, yet life thrives there.

Dr. Carl Woese and other scientists are taking x-ray photographs of individual ribonucleic acid (RNA) sections of thousands of different species. By comparing these x-ray photos, Woese is able to place each species on a new tree of life.

When the show aired, Woese was only a couple months from completing his tree of life of living things on earth (WGBH Educational Foundation and Clear Blue Sky Productions, Inc. 2001).

I stated that scientific facts belong to God. Based on his study of RNA, Woese stated that the theory of evolution would soon become a scientific fact, if it were not already so. Prominent scientists declare that evolution has most certainly obtained the rating of scientific fact (Mayr 2001).

What was created on Day Five?

Day Five was the creation of a universal spiritual law that would eventually cause DNA to form and creatures to evolve here in the physical world.

God spoke the first "Let there be" of Day Five to a substance called the waters, which was nonmass energy.

Is evolution ruled by a higher law?

Scientists have long known that life on planet Earth began in the seas, and evolution ruled the day. Even so, don't you know in your heart that there had to be another law higher than evolution that guided the changes in creatures? That is exactly what God created on Day Five, a spiritual law.

Day Five was a spiritual law substance, or an image of God's will, just like all the other days. With this day, God created life throughout creation, not just the planet Earth. The waters, which brought forth the spiritual law substance of moving creatures and fowl, were not the same physical waters (H_2O) that brought forth life on our planet. If the waters were the same as our physical waters, God would have needed to create new laws for each planet where He chose to put life.

What were the gathered waters transformed into?

Gathered waters transformed into physical matter when God spoke the words "Let dry *land* appear." Physical matter was created in two forms, mass matter or dry *land*, which brought forth grass, herbs, and trees by the electromagnetic force and nonmass matter, which were the waters that brought forth moving creatures and fowl as spiritual law substance. Gravitons and neutrinos are two examples of nonmass matter.

What were the fowl?

This is a good place to discuss a confusing statement in the first "Let there be" of Day Five. Please notice the wording, "and fowl that may fly above the earth in the open firmament of heaven." You might assume that the word earth refers to our planet, and the open firmament of heaven refers to our sky.

God gave the name Earth to dry *land*. Dry *land* was all physical matter. We live in a universe of dry *land*; therefore, the name Earth also refers to the entire universe, not just our little planet.

In the same statement is the expression "open firmament of heaven." Open firmament of heaven was, and is, a spiritual dimension adjoining nonmass energy, also known as the waters.

On Day Two, firmament divided the waters above firmament from the waters below firmament. Therefore, firmament became attached to both types of waters. Firmament is a nonphysical spiritual substance, or spiritual space and energy.

Then on Day Three, the waters under firmament were first gathered together and then scattered to become dry *land*. The firmament that was attached to the waters under firmament were first stretched by the gathering of the waters and then curved in the explosion that created dry *land*.

The firmament that is attached to the nonmass matter is the open firmament of heaven and the home of fowl. You probably have already guessed that fowl were moving creatures' spirit beings. The firmament attached to mass matter is closed firmament of heaven and the place where the spirits of physical beings reside.

How were creatures created on earth?

Day Five began when God gave the name Seas to gathered waters. Names are spirit Word from God, which are received into the spirit side of those who receive name. Within the name Seas were all three "Let there be" statements of Day Five.

The first "Let there be" statement spoken on Day Five, found in Genesis 1:20-21, created the evening of Day Five. The creatures that were created were real but they were made of nonmass energy. They were not physical like we are, but God certainly saw them as real creatures. The morning was created when the creatures received a blessing from God, when He spoke the second "Let there be" of that day in Genesis 1:22-23.

This blessing gave the spiritual creatures the ability and authority to form physical images of themselves in earth, or in the physical universe. Development of life here on earth was controlled by spirit from spiritual law substance creatures in the waters (nonmass physical matter).

The spirits or forces, which cause DNA to form here on earth, didn't overcome the physical forces. They merely guided electromagnetic forces in the formation of DNA. Spirits from spiritual-law-substance creatures in the nonmass waters were invisible gravity-like forces.

Is there a spiritual life force?

Because of DNA evidence, scientists believe all life on earth came from a common source, or one living organism. They believe this because of the lack of scientific evidence of a universal life force. Day Five of creation is the source of life force.

It is my opinion that the same DNA evidence that convinces scientists that all life has one common ancestor is pointing to another conclusion. Spirit (life force) from the spiritual law substance that is the fifth day of creation caused the DNA of organisms to form in similar ways.

Spiritual law substance of Day Five was, and is, an impersonal universal law in the same manner as gravity, strong nuclear, weak nuclear, and the electromagnetic force are. One wouldn't expect an electron on the moon to be different from an electron on earth. Both electrons obey one law, the law of electromagnetism. All life in the universe obeys life force from Day Five (Creature Day).

If life was an accident and wasn't obeying an unseen law, surely there would have been other unrelated life forms created within the last 3.5 billion years of life on earth.

When (or if) we ever have a DNA sample from an alien species, scientists will probably tell us that the alien had originated from earth.

How did life evolve on Earth?

On the planet Earth, life evolved from microscopic organisms. Scientists say that occasionally, by chance, mistakes in DNA reproduction gave creatures a better chance of survival. Natural selection purified species' gene pools. This process of elimination is also known as "survival of the fittest" (Mayr 2001).

I am not disputing any of the preceding facts, but there was more to the process of evolution than meets the eye. Unseen forces from Day Five guided the process of DNA change. Those creatures whose DNA were created in line with spirit from spirit law substance in the nonmass waters had a better chance to survive.

> And God said, Let the earth bring forth the living creature after his kind, cattle, and creeping thing, and beast of the earth after his kind: and it was so.
>
> And God made the beast of the earth after his kind, and cattle after their kind, and every thing that creepeth upon the earth after his kind: and God saw that *it was* good.
>
> Genesis 1:24-25

This "Let there be" statement was not applied directly to earth (mass matter). It was applied to the spiritual law substance that was the creatures in the nonmass waters. The receiving of this Word caused Day Five to issue seed light upon creatures that were already formed in the physical universe. Seed light used the physical creatures' own energies to create minds.

Minds gave creatures the ability to visualize and image or, in other words, to think. These early minds were very primitive reactionary minds. Development of mind was a key element in the process of evolution.

Let's review Day Five. The first "Let there be" statement of Day Five created creatures in the nonmass energy called the waters as spiritual law substance. The second "Let there be" statement of Day Five caused images of the first creatures to be formed in the seas of the physical world. Lastly, the third "Let there be" statement of Day Five caused physical creatures to develop minds. Minds are spirit from the spiritual law substance in the nonphysical world and energies of the brain of physical creatures.

So what are we to think of the following Bible verse?

> And out of the ground the Lord God formed every beast of the field, and every fowl of the air; and brought *them* unto Adam to see what he would call them: and whatsoever Adam called every living creature, that *was* the name thereof.
>
> Genesis 2:19

First, this was during the time after the seventh day, which was after man of the Garden of Eden was formed. The man Adam was a living soul. Since Adam was a living soul, the name blessing he gave to the creatures was for the creation of souls. Souls gave higher law to the spirits of physical creature beings who were evolving.

God's spoken words created the spiritual law substance that was the fifth day; therefore, it was God that formed the creatures out of the ground (early life forms in earth). The creatures to whom Adam gave name blessings were the spirits of earthly creatures that were evolving because of the spoken Word of God.

Creatures' souls received information about changing environments through the minds of creatures. Spirit from the souls of creatures caused the DNA, which created offspring, to change in ways that caused the young of creatures to be born with characteristics that helped them adapt to their surroundings.

Can evolution be found in any Bible stories?

The evolution process can be clearly seen in the Book of Genesis where Jacob wanted to prosper at his father-in-law Laban's expense. Jacob used his knowledge of evolution to take advantage of his father-in-law in an agreement they had between the two of them.

Jacob was caring for Leban's livestock. In exchange, Jacob was to receive any young livestock that was born ring-streaked, speckled, or spotted. By changing the creatures' environment, Jacob caused their minds to transmit information to the souls of the creatures, which caused an increased number of the livestock's young to be born ring-streaked, speckled, and spotted to adapt to their new environment.

And Jacob took him rods of green poplar, and of the hazel and chestnut tree; and pilled white strakes in them, and made the white appear which *was* in the rods.

And he set the rods which he had pilled before the flocks in the gutters in the watering troughs when the flocks came to drink, that they should conceive when they came to drink.

And the flocks conceived before the rods, and brought forth cattle ring-streaked, speckled, and spotted.

And Jacob did separate the lambs, and set the faces of the flocks toward the ring-streaked, and all the brown in the flock of Laban; and he put his own flocks by themselves, and put them not unto Laban's cattle.

And it came to pass, whensoever the stronger cattle did conceive, that Jacob laid the rods before the eyes of the cattle in the gutters, that they might conceive among the rods.

But when the cattle were feeble, he put *them* not in: so the feebler were Laban's, and the stronger Jacob's.

And the man increased exceedingly, and had much cattle, and maidservants, and menservants, and camels, and asses.

Genesis 30:37-43

Some would say that the changing of the livestock's colors and coat patterns was a miracle. I am not sure if it was a miracle or not. Because Jacob had favor with God, God revealed to him understanding of laws that He had placed in nature long ago. Jacob simply used his knowledge of God's laws to his advantage.

Did God speed up the process of evolution to bless Jacob? Maybe he did, but it is not certain. In any case, we still get a good picture of how the evolution process works.

Day Six

The Kingdom of Man

> And God said, Let us make man in our image, after our likeness: and let them have dominion over the fish of the sea, and over the fowl of the air, and over the cattle, and over all the earth, and over every creeping thing that creepth upon the earth.
>
> So God created man in his *own* image, in the image of God created he him; male and female created he them.
>
> Genesis 1:26-27

Were we really made in the image of God?

God is spirit and light and exists in the spiritual realm. He is the creator of the universe and all living things. We are flesh and bone, and Earth is our home. We have 99.9 percent of the same genes as chimpanzees, which indicates we are closely related (WGBH Educational Foundation and Clear Blue Sky Productions, Inc. 2001). Yet, the written Word of God informs us that we are made in God's image and after His likeness.

God's Word is truth. There is no need for believers to worry that if they search deep enough or think long enough they will prove that God's Word is faulty.

Day Six began when God gave the name Earth to dry *land*. The name Earth was spirit Word from God. Within the name Earth were the three "Let there be" statements concerning the Day of Man (Day Six).

How was Day Six created?

God's spoken words "Let us make man" combined with the substance of dry *land* (strong nuclear mass matter) to create the evening of the sixth day in the *image* and the *likeness* of God. The Day of Man, like the first five days, was created as spiritual law substance, or an image of God's will.

Before the first "Let there be" statement of Day Six could be spoken, it needed to receive something. The Word of God always needs faith before manifesting its works.

The faith needed for the manifestation of the three "Let there be" statements of the Day of Man was created when God's spoken words "Let the earth bring forth grass, the herb yielding seed, after his kind, and the tree yielding fruit, whose seed was in itself, after his kind" were obeyed; and dry *land* decayed into mass particles with electric charge to create electromagnetic force and neutrinos.

Neutrinos are particles without mass or charge, which can pass through earth and seldom be noticed. There are three types of neutrinos produced in association with electrons, muons, and tauons. Muons and tauons are heavy forms of electrons or excited states (Jones 1992).

The three types of neutrinos were used for faith to bring forth the three "Let there be" statements of Day Six. Neutrinos and dust of the earth must be the same thing.

What kind of dominion did man receive?

The second "Let there be" statement of Day Six, a dominion blessing, gave the spiritual law substance of Day Six the ability to rule over the earth's spiritual and physical universe. What does it mean to rule over all of the earth? Do you believe locusts would leave a farmer's field if the farmer would remind them that the blessing God gave to man on Day Six gave man dominion over every creeping thing that creepeth upon the earth? I don't think so.

The second "Let there be" statement of Day Six gave mankind a spiritual dominion over all the creatures. Man would judge the creatures to give them spiritual blessings (names).

Where is the third "Let there be" statement in Day Six?

And God blessed them, and God said unto them, Be fruitful, and multiply, and replenish the earth, and subdue it: and have dominion over the fish of the sea, and over the fowl of the air, and over every living thing that moveth upon the earth.

And God said, Behold, I have given you every herb bearing seed, which *is* upon the face of all the earth, and every tree, in the which *is* the fruit of a tree yielding seed; to you it shall be for meat.

And to every beast of the earth, and to every fowl of the air, and to every thing that creepeth upon the earth, wherein *there is* life, I *have given* every green herb for meat: and it was so.

Genesis 1:28-30

The blessing man received in Genesis 1:28-30 was the third "Let there be" statement of Day Six. We know it was a "Let there be" statement because when God blessed the creatures in Genesis 1:22, that was a "Let there be" statement.

The blessing received in Genesis 1:28-30 was a spiritual blessing that gave man another type of dominion over the creatures, which provided food for man and creatures.

Remember, all physical matter has a spirit side; therefore, there is both a physical place upon the face of all the earth and a spiritual place upon the face of all the earth. The Day of Man could not exercise its ability to rule until living soul man was formed.

Did God create man or did he evolve?

We don't know how man first came to be because we don't know what kind of man God created on Day Six, nor do we know the nature of the man that He placed within the Garden of Eden. The reason we lack knowledge about the kind of man He created on Day Six and the kind of man He formed to be placed in the Garden of Eden is because we don't know the true nature of a creation day. This lack of knowledge concerning a creation day would disappear if we had a better understanding of the Trinity and if we understood that the Trinity was the pattern for the creation of each of the creation days.

On Day Six God created man in His image and after His likeness. You probably heard this statement a countless number of times. In fact, I used this statement many times in this book, but the fact is that this statement is not completely correct. Let's look again at what God really said.

> And God said, Let us make man in our image, after our likeness...
>
> Genesis 1:26

When it came to the making of man, it was a team effort that got the job completed. God the Father, God the Son or Word, and God the Holy Spirit all had their part in the creation of man.

Leaving out the words "Let us" makes the statement easier to read and understand, but it also covers up an essential clue to how man was created.

In the second part of the first sentence in Genesis 1:26, it is written "in our image, after our likeness." Man was created in the image and in the likeness of God the Father, God the Son or Word, and God the Holy Spirit.

It is much easier to say that man was created in His image and after His likeness rather than in their image and after their likeness, but in doing this we lose two more essential clues to the mystery of the creation of man.

On Day Six, God the Father, God the Word, and God the Holy Spirit created man in their image and after their likeness. At that time, man did not have 99.9 percent of the same genes as a chimpanzee, but man was created as a creation day, or spiritual law substance.

Was God the pattern for creation days?

Each creation day had an evening, then a morning, and then, eventually, seed light or spirit and power were created. Surely God the Father, God the Word, and God the Holy Spirit were the pattern God used to create all of the creation days.

Evenings are the beginning of each day and they are a kind of father of each day. Before God the Father spoke anything into existence, He was complete and lacked nothing. God the Son or Word and God the Holy Spirit are part of God the Father and came from the Father. Mornings and seed light also originated from evenings, which are the father part of creation days.

The Son of God or the Word of God is the express image of God the Father (II Corinthians 4:4). God the Father is complete and is law unto Himself. God the Word is God the Father's law to others. They are opposites but still the same thing. God the Father is inward law to oneself; whereas, God the Son or Word is outward law to others.

Evenings and mornings are the opposite of each other but are still the same thing: a day. Mornings are the way evenings give their law to others. The Holy Spirit is the seed light or spirit and power of God the Father and God the Word. The Holy Spirit communicates the law of God to others. Seed light of a creation day communicates the law of a creation day to others.

Obeying the Holy Spirit causes those who obey to become images of God or sons of God. Obeying the seed light of a creation day allows one to become an image of that creation day. God first created man as Day Six, which was the law of God. Man of the Garden of Eden was created as an express image of Day Six, by seed light or spirit and power from Day Six. Remember, Day Six was an image of God's will, or God's Word.

What was created on Day Six?

On Day Six, by speaking three "Let there be" statements, God did not create living soul man of the Garden of Eden but rather He created spiritual law substance, or an image of God's will, with the power and instruction to create living soul man. At this point in creation, God had not yet formed the man that He would be placing in the Garden of Eden, nor had man received name from God. Also man had not yet given name to living creatures.

The third "Let there be" statement of Day Six (a food blessing) was not enforced until man was removed from the Garden of Eden. While man was in the Garden, he had permission to eat of every tree except for the tree of the knowledge of good and evil.

Are creation days dimensions?

According to my hypothesis, the three "Let there be" statements spoken on Day Three created our universe, which I call the Earth Universe. What about the other creation days, are they dimensions? Yes, but they are not all the same. Creation days one through three are substance dimensions, which form the foundations for the three levels of creation. Days four through seven are kingdom dimensions, which rule over the substance dimension.

Dimensions are arranged in a hierarchy according to their power and authority. The dimension that was created on Day Three (dry *land*) is influenced by other creation days, which I call kingdom dimensions.

How do we know this? According to Genesis 1:26, Day Five ruled over the waters (nonmass energy) to bring forth the moving creatures. This tells us that Day Five's (Kingdom of Creatures) must be a higher dimension than the waters, which is the evening part of Day Three.

When I say higher dimension, I mean the energy of that dimension is more pure in God's eye than the one I was comparing it to.

Man of the Garden of Eden, or Day Six, was formed of the dust of the earth and was given rule over the creatures and over all the earth (Genesis 1:26). This tells us that Day Six, or the kingdom-of-man dimension, is a higher dimension than the creature dimension of Day Five and the dry-*land* dimension of Day Three.

Creation days three, five, and six formed the third level of creation, which is the lowest level.

Day Four's dimension (lights in the firmament) and Day Two's dimension (firmament) are higher-level dimensions than Day Six, Day Five, and Day Three. Day Four's dimension (lights in the firmament) shined upon the earth to create signs, seasons, days, and years. Since man is ruled by signs, seasons, days, and years we know that Day Four's dimension is at a higher level than both Day Three (dry *land* dimension) and Day Six (man dimension).

Also, since Day Four's dimension was formed of the waters above firmament and then placed in the firmament of heaven, we know that Day Four's dimension is also at a higher level than Day Two (firmament dimension).

Creation days two and four formed the second level of creation or the Kingdom of Lights, which we know as the Kingdom of Heaven.

Day One's light was separated from the darkness and given the name "Day" to bring forth the seventh day which became the Kingdom of God.

Obviously, Day Seven is higher than any other dimension, including the dimension of light that was created on Day One.

Days one and seven, plus the presence of God, formed the first level of creation, which is the highest level of creation. (See Appendix C)

I would like to describe in detail what each dimension and level of creation is like but I can't. I don't know their true nature, but there are some clues.

Each creation day has an evening, a morning, and a seed light. Could there be three dimensions within each creation day, or are evenings, mornings, and seed light just properties of each creation day? The universe we live in was created with the three "Let there be" statements of Day Three and influences from other creation days. We call this reality we live in a universe, but in the bigger picture, our Day Three universe is just another dimension in God's creation.

How do dimensions interact?

In the beginning of this book, I claimed that creation days were not periods of time but were, in fact, created things. Then I introduced the concept that the creation days were spiritual law substances, or images of God's will. Later, I presented my belief that the creation days were and are dimensions, connected together in a hierarchy by levels of power and authority.

I don't believe they force their will upon other dimensions. They only provide unseen, undetectable gravity-like forces to guide and shape the energy matter of other dimensions that will yield to their authority and power. This is why many scientists say they see no evidence of influence from unseen worlds. Scientists are trying to find unseen, undetectable gravity-like forces, which makes their task extremely hard and maybe impossible.

Einstein said, "I want to know God's thoughts." He was speaking of understanding the fundamental laws of physics and how they all came to be. Mr. Einstein was working from the bottom to the top or from what was known to the scientists to what was unknown.

My mental capacity is not at all on the same par as Mr. Einstein's. I could not play the game by using his rules, but I too wanted to know the thoughts of God. Therefore, I started at the top and worked toward the bottom. That is, I started with the "Let there be" statements in Chapter 1 of Genesis and worked to what is already known to scientists.

What I have presented in this book concerning the seven days of creation is only my hypothesis, but I really believe it is the truth. I cannot prove scientifically that there are three levels of creation nor can I prove that each creation day created its own dimension, but I do have "peace." I can now understand how all creation fits neatly together. I thank God for His "thoughts" which He first spoke to create everything and then spoke to His prophets.

Theories of everything are concerned with how all the fundamental laws of physics came together to create our universe. These theories start out with what can be proved and then end up with what they hope to prove in the future. My hypothesis starts with the written Word and ends with what I believe the written Word means.

A seven-dimension-super-string theory is one popular theory, which scientists hope will lead them to the final truth concerning the creation of the universe. Personally, I'm convinced that those who are pursuing this particular theory are on the right track, and the seven dimensions they speak of correspond with the seven-day dimensions that are the subject of this book.

Because of the information God has placed in the Bible, it is possible to understand creation as seven-day dimensions that were placed in three levels according to their energy level and authority. Each creation day can be thought of as a dimension in creation.

Part III

Day Seven and Beyond

Day Seven

The Kingdom of God

Thus the heavens and the earth were finished, and all the host of them.

And on the seventh day God ended his work which he had made; and he rested on the seventh day from all his work which he had made.

And God blessed the seventh day, and sanctified it: because that in it he had rested from all his work which God created and made.

Genesis 2:1-3

Christians worship God the Father, God the Son, and God the Spirit or Holy Ghost. These three are one in God. Let us examine the Trinity.

On Day One, God gave the name Day to light in order to create the seventh day. On the other six days of creation, when God wanted to create an evening, a morning, or seed light from a day, He said something like "Let there be." There are no "Let there be" statements written in the Bible for the seventh day. However, I still believe there were an evening, a morning, and a seed light from that day.

When God rested on and then in the seventh day it was evening. When He blessed the seventh day it was morning. Finally, the sanctification of the seventh day was a dividing of seed light from that day.

Why didn't God say, "Let there be," on the seventh day? He probably planned to speak these words in the future when circumstances were right. God didn't speak the third "Let there be" statement of Day Five until He was ready to create Day Six. Man of Day Six was needed to name earth's living creatures of Day Five. Patience is a good thing.

Why would God wait to speak a "Let there be" statement? There are two parts to each "Let there be" statement, which are not to be confused with the three "Let there be" statements in each day. When God first speaks a word to someone, or something, that word is a calling. Within the name from God are all the power, authority, and ability to become the thing God wants it to be. Sometimes God waits until the circumstances are right before He speaks a "Let there be" statement.

The second part of a "Let there be" statement is the judgment of the work done by the first part of a "Let there be" statement. God waits for fruit to develop before He judges it to be good or bad. This part of the "Let there be" statement can be clearly seen in the first chapter of the Bible. God would speak a "Let there be" statement and then it would be followed by an "And God made" statement or an "And God saw" statement, which were judgments.

Is the Word God's Son?

God said He was finished with His work, but what exactly had He made? The creative words that God spoke in order to create the first seven days came from His heart. Could God's creative words have been His Son?

> In the beginning was the Word, and the Word was with God, and the Word was God.
> The same was in the beginning with God.
> All things were made by him; and without him was not any thing made that was made.
> In him was life; and the life was the light of men.
>   John 1:1-4

These verses make it sound like the Word was in fact the creative words God spoke. Could all the "Let there be" statements and names given by God be manifestations of God?

Let's look at Jesus' own words about who He was at the time of creation.

> And unto the angel of the church of the Laodiceans write; These things saith the Amen, the faithful and true witness, *the beginning of the creation of God*;
>
> > Revelation 3:14
> > [*emphasis* added]

The seven days of creation were universal laws for all creation. These spiritual law substances were the manifestations of the Word of God and the substance of faith.

> Through *faith* we understand that the worlds were framed by *the word of God*, so that things which are seen were not made of things which do appear.
>
> > Hebrews 11:3
> > [*emphasis* added]

When God rested on and then in the seventh day, He was resting in His Son, or His Word. After He blessed the seventh day and sanctified it, God (The Word) went to work.

> These *are* the generations of the heavens and of the earth when they were created, in the day that the *Lord God* made the earth and the heavens,
>
> > Genesis 2:4
> > [*second emphasis* added]

The Lord God (The Word) began His work after God rested in Him.

Believest thou not that I am in the Father, and the Father in me? the words that I speak unto you I speak not of myself: but the Father that dwelleth in me, he doeth the works.

John 14:10

The Lord God used all seven days of creation and generations to do His works. Stars and planets come and go, but the universal law of God (The Word) remains constant. It is a Rock.

Is Jesus a created being?

Jesus Christ, the Word of God, came from His eternal Father; therefore, Jesus had to be eternal. When Jesus, as Word from His Father, manifested outside of God, He was *made* the spiritual universal law for creation from which came all the laws of physics.

Being *made* so much better than the angels, as he hath by inheritance obtained a more excellent name than they.

Hebrews 1:4
[*emphasis* added]

For by him were all things created, that are in heaven, and that are in earth, visible and invisible, whether *they be* thrones, or dominions, or principalities, or powers: all things were created by him, and for him:
And he is before all things, and by him all things consist.

Colossians 1:16-17

Who and what is Jesus?

In the preceding Bible verses we are told many things about Jesus. He was the beginning of God's creation, and was made better than the angels. He created all things, all things were created for Him, and He was before all things. Even now, by Him all things consist. Also,

Jesus was the Word of God and was God. Without Him nothing was made.

We are also told that through faith the Word of God framed the worlds. All of this information is in agreement with my hypothesis.

God's spoken Word, from which came all creation days, was indeed God's Son. When God said, "Let there be" and gave names, He was giving birth to His Son.

Jesus was within each of the creation days because He was the Word that created them. By the presence of Jesus, each day was and is upheld.

On the seventh day God rested on and then in His Son, and He blessed his Son with the seven spirits of life.

The idea that Jesus was the spoken Word of God is not new. This is shown in the first chapter of the Book of Genesis. A second century author, Athenagaras of Athens, presented a similar hypothesis to his readers (Zannoni 1994).

What is God's right hand?

The seven name spirits that God used to create the first seven days of creation could be considered God's left hand. Creation days are impersonal. From the creation days flowed the laws of physics that created our universe. As you know, the laws of physics are also impersonal.

It is easy to believe that things like darkness, light, waters, firmament, gathered waters, and dry *land* were impersonal, but what about living creatures and man?

Living beings are created with both left-hand spirit law and right-hand spirit law. Our bodies are created with impersonal laws and our bodies are ruled by right-hand spirit, which is our life spirit.

Right-hand name spirit was introduced on the seventh day of creation when God blessed the seventh day.

> Thus the heavens and the earth were finished, and all the host of them.
>
> And on the seventh day God ended his work which he had made; and he rested on the seventh day from all his work which he had made.
>
> And God blessed the seventh day, and sanctified it: because that in it he had rested from all his work which God created and made.
>
> Genesis 2:1-3

God blessed the seventh day with His own presence. When the seventh day was blessed, seven right-hand name spirits went forth to give life to God's creation.

Jesus has all seven of these spirits.

> And I beheld, and, lo, in the midst of the throne and of the four beasts, and in the midst of the elders, stood a Lamb as it had been slain, having seven horns and seven eyes, which are the seven Spirits of God sent forth into all the earth.
>
> Revelation 5:6

What can name spirit do?

The receiving of name from God has led to many great things in history. Abram was called Abraham, which means father of many nations, before he became the father.

> Neither shall thy name any more be called Abram, but thy name shall be Abraham; for a father of many nations have I made thee.
>
> Genesis 17:5

Before Sarai had children, she was given the name of Sarah, which means mother of nations.

And God said unto Abraham, As for Sarai thy wife, thou shalt not call her name Sarai, but Sarah *shall* her name *be*.

And I will bless her, and give thee a son also of her: yea, I will bless her, and she shall be *a mother* of nations; kings of people shall be of her.

Genesis 17:15-16

Adam also named his wife before she conceived children.

And Adam called his wife's name Eve; because she was the mother of all living.

Genesis 3:20

The name Sarah proceeded from the name Abraham, and the name Eve proceeded from the name Adam. What does this mean?

When Abraham called his wife Sarah, spiritual substance was removed from Abraham's spirit being and added to his wife's spirit being. The name Sarah gave Abraham's wife the authority and power to become a mother of nations and kings (Genesis 17:15-16).

Earlier in history, Adam gave part of his name to his wife. Spiritual substance was removed from Adam's spirit and placed within his wife's spirit. Because she was named Eve, Adam's wife became the mother to all living (Genesis 3:20).

In another example, God gave the name Israel to Jacob in order to create the nation of Israel.

And God said unto him, Thy name *is* Jacob: thy name shall not be called any more Jacob, but Israel shall be thy name: and he called his name Israel.

And God said unto him, I *am* God Almighty: be fruitful and multiply; a nation and a company of nations shall be of thee, and kings shall come out of thy loins;

Genesis 35:10-11

Name from God gives the receiver of the name the ability to give faith back to God. Faith is needed to receive the promises of God.

Is name spirit valuable?

Modern man has lost the knowledge of name blessings from God. Jacob and his mother Rebecca knew the importance of name blessings. They used trickery to receive the blessing that Esau was to receive from Isaac. Isaac received his blessing from Abraham, who had received it from God.

As mentioned earlier, Jacob also received the name blessing of Israel from God. The name blessing of Israel was for the making of the nation of Israel, other nations, and kings.

The ancient people of the land of Shinar, who built the Tower of Babel, most certainly knew the importance of name blessings. They were willing to build a city and a tower whose top could reach into heaven in order to make them a name.

> And they said one to another, Go to, *let us* make brick, and burn them thoroughly. And they had brick for stone, and slime had they for mortar.
> And they said, Go to, *let us* build us a city and a tower, whose top *may reach* unto heaven; and *let us* make us a name, lest we be scattered abroad upon the face of the whole earth.
> Genesis 11:3-4
> [first, second, and fourth *emphasis* added]

Notice that "let us" is used three times in these verses. Does this remind you of the three "Let there be" statements that God used to make each creation day? These people were trying to receive a name to create their own day, or kingdom. After all, isn't each creation day really a kingdom?

As the people were building a city and a tower, they were obeying the three "let us" statements they had spoken. Somehow the knitting together of their souls and their hearts created one spiritual language or spirit force. These ancient people were developing real spiritual power.

The people of Shinar received the name of Babel from God. Babel was not the name they wanted. God found a way to stop them before they received a name that would allow them to do anything they imagined to do. And the Lord came down to see the city and the tower, which the children of men had built.

> And the Lord said, Behold, the people *is* one, and they have all one language; and this they begin to do: and now nothing will be restrained from them, which they have imagined to do.
> Go to, let us go down, and there confound their language, that they may not understand one another's speech.
> So the Lord scattered them abroad from thence upon the face of all the earth: and they left off to build the city.
> Therefore is the name of it called Babel; because the Lord did there confound the language of all the earth: and from thence did the Lord scatter them abroad upon the face of all the earth.
>
> Genesis 11:5-9

God confounded their spiritual language or their spiritual oneness. The physical language they spoke was divided before they built the tower.

> By these were the isles of the Gentiles divided in their lands; every one after his tongue, after their families, in their nations.
>
> Genesis 10:5

> These are the sons of Shem, after their families, after their tongues, in their lands, after their nations. These are the families of the sons of Noah, after their generations, in their nations: and by these were the nations divided in the earth after the flood.
>
> Genesis 10:31-32

After receiving the name of Babel, the people of Shinar were able to build a kingdom. Nimrod was the founder of that kingdom.

> And Cush begat Nimrod: he began to be a mighty one in the earth.
> He was a mighty hunter before the Lord: wherefore it is said, Even as Nimrod the mighty hunter before the Lord.
> And the beginning of his kingdom was Babel, and Erech, and Accad, and Calneh, in the land of Shinar.
>
> Genesis 10:8-10

Where does the power in name spirit come from?

Those who receive Jesus as Lord and Savior receive a new spirit and a new heart. That's what a name spirit is: spirit and heart.

Christians that obey their new spirit cause Christ to form in their new hearts. Christ is the power of God. Speaking words from a Christ-filled heart releases the power of God to work in the believers' lives.

Whenever God names a person, they receive a new spirit and a new heart, just like a new believer in Jesus receives a new spirit and a new heart. Obeying their new spirit causes Christ to form in their new heart. Speaking words from their Christ-filled heart releases the power of God to accomplish God's will.

In answer to the question where does the power of name spirit come from, it comes from the power of God within their new hearts, which comes from Christ, the power of God, and the wisdom of God (1 Corinthians 1:24).

Does God name people today?

God calls or names people all over this world to do the work of His will. Usually, God speaks to their spirit. Sometimes people can hear their names being called audibly.

On a personal note, both my wife and I have heard our names called in an audible voice on several occasions. I hold the belief that God has given me a name to understand the Bible in a different light than most people. My wife Kathleen also received an anointing to help me write, which I am very thankful for, because I would be lost without her anointed help.

Do I think I have all the right answers? Of course not, but again, the most anointed preachers in the land are not always right either. They are anointed or named by God to fulfill the purpose God gave them to do. They just have to do the best they can.

Have you ever heard your name called to serve God? Over the years I have met many others who have also heard their names called audibly. They range from preachers to factory workers.

What are revelations?

The hunger for the written Word God gave to me caused the Word of God to be stored in my new heart, as I studied the Bible. Then as I was meditating on his Word, God would reveal from my heart the words that I needed in order to receive understanding.

The revelations that I received were nothing more than the word I placed in my heart through studying and meditating on the Word of God. Then when I needed it, the Holy Spirit would give me the answers to my questions.

Do you remember when Jesus asked the disciples who they thought He was? Then Peter replied that Jesus was the Christ, the Son of God (Matthew 16:16)? God had revealed it to him at that time, but Peter had already been told that Jesus was the Christ (John 1:40-42). So revelations, most of the time, are information that is stored in the mind and then revealed by the Holy Spirit. This is not always the case, however, sometimes revelations are new information from God.

Living Soul Man

Why do men have physical bodies?

In the past I have heard preachers say that we were created with a physical body in order to rule the earth that the Lord gave to man. Why do we need a physical body to rule the earth? God is a Spirit with a spirit body and rules over all creation that He created. If God doesn't need a physical body to accomplish His work, why do we need a physical body to rule over the earth? Aren't we created in His image and after His likeness?

Before Jesus came to the physical earth He was in the form of God and equal with God.

> Let this mind be in you, which was also in Christ Jesus:
> Who, being in the form of God, thought it not robbery to be equal with God:
> But made himself of no reputation, and took upon him the form of a servant, and was made in the likeness of men:
> Philippians 2:5-7

When Jesus left heaven, He was eventually made in the likeness of man, which included having a physical body. Since man was created in God's image and after God's likeness, shouldn't man have been created with a spiritual body in the likeness of God?

In Philippians 2:6 it is written that before Jesus came in the flesh to the earth, He was in the form of God and was equal with God. Jesus was on the earth, and He was the Word of God (John 1:1). Jesus Christ is the express image of God the Father (II Corinthians 4:4). Wouldn't God also be some kind of Word? It does follow reason that both the Son and the Father would be of the same nature.

Jesus Christ is the Son of God and the Word of God. Father God is most likely some kind of Word. God's own written words say "Let us make man in our image after our likeness. . ." (Genesis 1:26). Why wouldn't God have created man as some kind of "word" who was an image of God the Father, God the Son, and God the Holy Spirit?

The man God created on Day Six was created in the image and in the likeness of God the Father, God the Son, and God the Holy Spirit. Man was created as spiritual law substance, which was the image of God's will. He was an image of God's Word; therefore, man was also a type of "word."

Where was the Garden of Eden located?

God created the man He would place in the Garden of Eden sometime after Day Six.

> And the Lord God planted a garden eastward in Eden;
> and there he put the man whom he had formed.
>
> Genesis 2:8

Living soul man of the Garden of Eden was the bridge between the spiritual law substance created on Day Six and physical man here in the physical world.

The Garden of Eden must have been one very strange place. We know by reading the Bible that there were at least one talking snake, trees with spiritual power, naked people, and the voice of God walking in the evening. The Garden of Eden sounds more like a spiritual place than a physical place.

People have spent a lot of time and money looking for the Garden of Eden. When God removed man from the Garden, He didn't destroy it. God placed cherubim and a flaming sword at the east end to keep the way of the tree of life.

So he drove out the man; and he placed at the east of the garden of Eden Cherubims, and a flaming sword which turned every way, to keep the way of the tree of life.

> Genesis 3:24

Somewhere, the Garden of Eden is at peace, under guard, in the same location as it was way back in the beginning.

And a river went out of Eden to water the garden; and from thence it was parted, and became into four heads.

The name of the first *is* Pison: that *is* it which compasseth the whole land of Havilah, where *there is* gold;

And the gold of that land *is* good: there *is* bdellium and the onyx stone.

And the name of the second river *is* Gihon: the same *is* it that compasseth the whole land of Ethiopia.

And the name of the third river *is* Hiddekel: that *is* it which goeth toward the east of Assyria. And the fourth river *is* Euphrates.

> Genesis 2:10-14

God's written words in Genesis do not completely correspond with information concerning physical rivers here in the earth. God's Word is truth; therefore, we can assume the rivers are spiritual in nature, meaning the Garden of Eden was a spiritual place.

Some day the city of New Jerusalem will come down from heaven.

And he carried me away in the spirit to a great and high mountain, and showed me that great city, the holy Jerusalem, *descending out of heaven from God,*

> Revelation 21:10
> [*emphasis* added]

The tree of life will be within this city from heaven.

> In the midst of the street of it, and on either side of the
> river, *was there* the tree of life, which bare twelve *manner* of
> fruits, *and* yielded her fruit every month: and the leaves of the
> tree *were* for the healing of the nations.
>
> Revelation 22:2

We know the tree of life was in the midst of the Garden of Eden;
therefore, the Garden must have been somewhere in heaven.

In the Book of Revelation, Jesus said the tree of life was located
in the midst of the paradise of God.

> He that hath an ear, let him hear what the Spirit saith unto
> the churches; To him that overcometh will I give to eat of the
> tree of life, which is *in the midst of the paradise of God.*
>
> Revelation 2:7
> [*emphasis* added]

Paul tells of a man he knew who was caught up to the third
heaven.

> I knew a man in Christ above fourteen years ago,
> (whether in the body, I cannot tell; or whether out of the body,
> I cannot tell: God knoweth;) such an one caught up to *the third
> heaven.*
>
> II Corinthians 12:2
> [*emphasis* added]

Paul calls the third heaven paradise.

> How that he was caught up into *paradise,* and heard
> unspeakable words, which it is not lawful for a man to utter.
>
> II Corinthians 12:4
> [*emphasis* added]

The third heaven sounds like a place where one might find a talking snake, trees with spiritual power, naked people, the voice of God walking in the evening, cherubim, and a flaming sword. The Garden of Eden was a spiritual place created for spiritual beings. After all, God is a spirit being. Why would He create His garden here on the physical earth? If you were going to make a garden, wouldn't you plant it where you lived? If God planted His garden in physical earth, wouldn't that be like us planting our garden in hell?

The Garden of Eden was located within the name Earth, which was a spiritual heaven. There are seven spiritual heavens. They were created when God gave the name Night to darkness, the name Seas to gathered waters, the name Earth to dry *land*, the name Heaven to firmament, a Spirit of God to void, another Spirit of God to face of waters, and the name Day to light. Remember, these names are all Spirit Word from God and are part of God. All heavens were created for spirit beings.

When was living soul man created?

Armed with the knowledge of what God created on Day Six (Day of Man) and where and what the Garden of Eden was, we are now able to begin to understand the process of the creation of living soul man. The following Bible verse offers proof that living soul man (Garden of Eden man) had yet to be created.

> And every plant of the field *before it was in the earth*, and every herb of the field before it grew: for the Lord God had not caused it to rain upon the earth, and *there was* not a man to till the ground.
>
> Genesis 2:5
[first emphasis added]

Why would God say He had not caused it to rain upon the earth? Every scientist and farmer knows there has to be rain upon our planet before grass, herbs, and trees will grow. Since the man that God created next was a spirit man in a spirit place (Garden of Eden), doesn't it make sense that the rain and plants of the field, upon the earth, were all spirit in nature? Living soul man was needed to give spiritual blessing or rain (name blessing) to the plants.

As people here on earth, we naturally think the whole face of the ground was the ground we walked upon, but that's only half of the truth. Just like we humans are both physical and spiritual, so is the ground. Spirit plants were waiting on the spirit side of the ground for the time when man would till the ground spiritually. Genesis 2:5 is about spirit plants on the spirit side of the earth. The phrases "before it was in earth" and "before it grew" support this hypothesis.

How was living soul man created?

The physical world's spirit dimensions were created when God gave the name Earth to dry *land* and the name Seas to the gathered waters. These spirit places were created for the Day of Creature and the Day of Man, which were creation days five and six.

> And the Lord God formed man *of* the dust of the ground, and breathed into his nostrils the breath of life; and man became a living soul.
>
> Genesis 2:7

Man's body was formed by spirit from the Day of Man. God gave man the name Adam, which became the breath of life to man, or man's life spirit. Remember that Day Six was the spiritual law substance, or the image of God's will, that manifested from the Word of God and faith and was part of the being of the Lord God.

Man became a living soul only after the Lord God breathed the breath of life into his nostrils. The breath of life was not oxygen. Oxygen belonged to the physical world, and since God is a Spirit, His breath of life must have been spirit in nature. Ask any mother of a newborn baby and they will tell you that their baby was most definitely alive before taking their first breath (Job 27:3).[10] The breath that God breathed into man's nostrils was a name spirit called Adam.

The name spirit called Adam caused the man to develop mind, soul, and heart. The name Adam came from God and was God. When man received the name Adam from God he became a spiritual living soul.

Here in the earth we think of dust as dirt without water that the wind has caused to raise into the air. That's a good place to start, but if we are to know the truth about the creation of man, we need a deeper understanding of what dust is.

As mentioned earlier, God's spoken words, "Let the earth bring forth grass, the herb yielding seed, and the fruit tree. .," caused dry *land* particles to decay into particles with electric charge. In the process, some energy was released as dust. The force of gravity had little or no effect on them. It is my guess that the dust from which God formed man's body was neutrinos.

Remember that neutrinos are uncharged elementary particles that came in three forms, one for each "Let there be" statement of Day Six (Day of Man). But of course I'm only hypothesizing.

Why was Adam in a spiritual place?

The man of the Garden of Eden was an image of Day Six. The Garden of Eden was to be man's habitat, not the physical earth. Why wasn't man to be here in the physical earth? I know of two good reasons. First, man was created for companionship with God, and since the Garden of Eden was a spirit place, man would have been closer to God's presence there than he would have been if he were on the physical earth. We know this is true because of what Cain said.

> Behold, thou hast driven me out this day from the face of
> the earth; and from thy face shall I be hid; . . .
>
> Genesis 4:14

If God had driven Cain from the physical face of the earth, Cain would have been in outer space somewhere.

The second reason man was not created in the physical earth is the most important one. The law substance of man was created in the image and after the likeness of God. God is spirit, not physical flesh; therefore, man of the Garden of Eden, who was an image of the sixth day of creation, was created with spiritual flesh. Man did not become physical flesh until after the fall from the Garden.

> *There are* also celestial bodies, and bodies terrestrial: but the glory of the celestial *is* one, and the *glory* of the terrestrial *is* another.
>
> I Corinthians 15:40

Was living soul man different from man on earth?

Living soul man was created in the image of God after His likeness. Adam could stand in the presence of God and carry on a conversation. How awesome that must have been!

Do you find it hard to believe that living soul man of the Garden of Eden could have been something other than a physical man here upon the earth? Would you like proof that living soul man was not the same as physical man here on earth? If you are a man, stop shaving for about a week and then stand in front of a mirror. You will see a creature staring back at you that has 99.9 percent of the same genes as a chimpanzee. Man shares distant ancestors with apes (WGBH Educational Foundation and Clear Blue Sky Productions, Inc. 2001).

Living soul man was created in the image of God after His likeness, and God is a Spirit. That in my opinion makes living soul man a spiritual being.

Man here on earth is the spiritual image and likeness of living soul man, but our physical bodies are in the image and likeness of earth's living creatures.

Living soul man of the Garden of Eden was of the man species. After man was removed from the Garden as seed light from Day Six, he was made available to earthly man. The son-of-man species, or modern man, was the result of this union.
Note the following Bible verses.

How much less man, *that is* a worm? and the son of man, *which is* a worm?

Job 25:6

Lord, what *is* man, that thou takest knowledge of him! *or* the son of man, that thou makest account of him!

Psalms 144:3

These Bible verses are strong evidence in support of the existence of the son-of-man species.

To those who think it is unbelievable for God to mix man and beast in order to create the son-of-man species, look to Jeremiah for what God did to create the son-of-God species.

Behold, the days come, saith the Lord, that I will sow the house of Israel and the house of Judah with the seed of man, and with the seed of beast.

Jeremiah 31:27

Jesus Christ is the seed of the house of Israel and the house of Judah, and the seed of man and the seed of beast is the son-of-man species.

And I will bring forth a seed out of Jacob, and out of Judah an inheritor of my mountains: and mine elect shall inherit it, and my servants shall dwell there.

Isaiah 65:9

When King David was alive, he knew he had to die and be raised from the dead in order to be recreated in the likeness of God.

> As for me, I will behold thy face in righteousness: I shall be satisfied, when I awake, with thy likeness.
>
> Psalms 17:15

Did our bodies come from beasts?

> I said in mine heart concerning the estate of the sons of men, that God might manifest them, and that they might see that they themselves are beasts.
>
> Ecclesiastes 3:18

I pray that God will grant King Solomon's wish. The wisest man who ever lived spoke these words. Who am I to disagree with him?

We know King Solomon's thoughts concerning the true identity of man on earth, but what about God's thoughts? Did God leave any clues about the identity of man in His written Word? Evidence to the affirmative can be found in Chapter Ten of the Book of Acts.

God showed Peter in a vision that all mankind were candidates for salvation.

> And saw heaven opened, and a certain vessel descending unto him, as it had been a great sheet knit at four corners, and let down to earth:
> Wherein were all manner of fourfooted beasts of the earth, and wild beasts, and creeping things, and fowls of the air.
>
> Acts 10:11-12

These verses clearly show mankind represented by the four types of creatures. God could have used four nationalities of men, but he didn't. It therefore seems logical that God was revealing his secrets to those who would seek understanding concerning man's origins in the future.

What about contradicting Bible verses?

I have hypothesized that man was created in a spiritual place first. What about the Bible verses that seem to contradict such a hypothesis?

Let's examine some of the more challenging verses.

> Knowest thou *not* this of old, since man was placed upon earth,
>
> Job 20:4

Man was placed upon the earth. Living soul man Adam was placed upon the spirit side of the earth to be seed light to the earth's living creatures. As the result of the union between man's seed light and earth's living creatures, the son-of-man species was created.

> In the sweat of thy face shalt thou eat bread, till thou return unto the ground; for out of it wast thou taken: for dust thou *art*, and unto dust shalt thou return.
>
> Genesis 3:19

This verse reminds me of a man I once met at a Laundromat who had taught Sunday school for many years. He made a statement that shocks me to this very day. He said that when one reads the Bible, one should always take the most obvious meaning and never look for a deeper meaning. I have always thought receiving understanding from the Scriptures is like peeling an onion. Underneath each layer of understanding there can be found yet a deeper meaning. This verse can clearly be used to describe both a modern man and Adam, if he was also physical.

Could this same Bible verse allow for a spiritual Adam? Yes, I think so. The man Adam was formed of the dust of the earth. I believe the dust was neutrinos; but whatever the dust was, it was made on Day Three. When Adam was removed from the Garden of Eden, he returned to the place from which his substance came. That doesn't mean that he was created from the same substance as modern man.

Man left the Garden of Eden as seed light from Day Six (Day of Man). Man became higher spiritual law to the creatures. He had to work hard for his living. Have you ever tried to get an animal to behave like a person?

Let's look at another Bible verse.

And it repented the Lord that he had made man on the earth, and it grieved him at his heart.

Genesis 6:6

God did make man on earth. God formed living soul man out of the dust of the earth and placed him in the Garden of Eden, which is on spiritual earth.

God also made physical man on earth. He used seed light from the Day of Man and physical creatures here on the earth to make man on the earth.

When you come across Bible verses that seem to contradict my hypothesis, pray, search the Scriptures, and meditate on them.

Man's Evolution

The third "Let there be" statement for the creation of creatures (Let the earth bring forth the living creature) created seed light. After becoming anointed with name from Adam, this anointed seed light shined into the spirits of creatures already living on earth, which caused the creatures to evolve first spiritually and then physically. One of the creatures that evolved was early man. This is why chimpanzees have 99.9 percent of the same genes as humans.

When man left the Garden of Eden, he left as anointed seed light from Day Six (Day of Man). Man shined into the spiritual bodies of physical creatures (early man). Early man developed higher spiritual bodies that were capable of receiving the name Adam.

Are Christians evolving?

This procedure should not surprise Christians. After all, we received Light of Christ within our spirit being in order for us to develop a higher spirit being. Our old spirit being could not hold the Holy Spirit.

Consider this. When Jesus came to the earth, He didn't bring along His spiritual body, but He put on an earthly human body. Jesus came to give light to mankind so they could become son-of-God species. Man came as seed light from Day Six to give light to the creatures so they could become son-of man species because Satan had purchased mankind.

Can contradicting Bible verses be explained?

If the man, Adam, of the Garden of Eden was not physical like us, but a spiritual living soul, what are we to make of the following Bible verses?

> And so it is written, The first man Adam was made a living soul; the last Adam *was made* a quickening spirit.
> Howbeit that *was* not first which is spiritual, but that which is natural; and afterward that which is spiritual.
> The first man *is* of the earth, earthy: the second man *is* the Lord from heaven.
> As *is* the earthy, such *are* they also that are earthy: and as *is* the heavenly, such *are* they also that are heavenly.
> And as we have borne the image of the earthy, we shall also bear the image of the heavenly.
>
> I Corinthians 15: 45-49

God's Word is truth, but our understanding of His Word may not be complete. The challenge is to find the true meaning of God's Word.

When Paul wrote that the first man is of the earth and earthy, he was saying that both Adam's body and ours are made of physical material, nonheavenly material that was created on Day Three. He was not saying that Adam's body and our bodies were created of the exact same substance, because they were not.

We are made in the image and likeness of the man Adam. The first Adam was created in the image and in the likeness of God. The man, Adam, was created with the dust of the earth (energy that had risen above our universe). He was not created with the same substance that formed God, and we were not created with the same substance as the first man Adam. When I say that the first man Adam was a spiritual living soul and not physical, I mean that he was made with energy other than the kind of energy things are made of in this universe. First man Adam was spiritual in comparison to our physical universe, but if we would compare Adam to the heavenly universe, he would be of the earth and earthly.

When Paul said that the second man is the Lord from heaven, he was talking about God giving man the breath of life. The breath of life that God gave to man was the name Adam. The name Adam is from God and is God. That is why Paul said that the second man is the Lord from heaven.

The name Adam caused man to develop mind, soul, and heart. Later, the last Adam (Jesus) was made a quickening Spirit to be received in the hearts of His believers to make images of Jesus Christ in their spirit beings. As Paul said, we have borne the image of the earthly (Adam), we shall also bear the image of the heavenly (Jesus Christ).

Those who bear the image of Jesus Christ in their spirit man will someday bear His image in heaven, for they shall be like Jesus.

Beloved, now are we the sons of God, and it doth not yet appear what we shall be: but we know that, when he shall appear, *we shall be like him;* for we shall see him as he is.

I John 3:2
[*emphasis* added]

Why did Paul word these verses in a way that was so hard to understand? It was probably the same reason that God made the creation days seem like periods of time and probably the same reason that the Old Testament was written in a way that the Jews would not believe Jesus was the Christ, the Son of God. It seems to me that God sets up stumbling blocks so His servants have to study, meditate, and pray for revelations.

Why was man naked in the Garden?

And they were both naked, the man and his wife, and were not ashamed.

Genesis 2:25

Why was it shameful for Adam and Eve to be naked after their eyes were opened but not before?

As Christians, we are to have childlike faith, but not childlike understanding. Man and woman of the Garden of Eden were the fruit of Day Six (Day of Man). They were made in the image and in the likeness of Day Six.

Every day of creation had an evening, a morning, and a dividing of light from that day to upon another day. Light of a day was Word of that day. Word or light from a day was law and authority of that day. The receivers of light from another day could use the light or law to improve themselves, but if they used light belonging to another day, the user had to give glory to the day from which the light came. The glory they earned was clothing.

When man and woman were in the Garden of Eden there was no light or law going out from the Day of Man to any other day, because God had not yet judged living soul man. No light going out meant no glory was coming in, and that meant no clothing, thus, nakedness. As soon as man and woman ate of the fruit of the tree of knowledge of good and evil, which belonged to Day Five (Day of Creature), they knew they were naked.

Adam and Eve sewed fig leaves together to make themselves aprons (Genesis 3:7).[11] Chances are, the fig leaves were a type of glory belonging to God for the use of the blessing He gave to man.

> And God said, Behold, I have given you every herb bearing seed, which *is* upon the face of all the earth, and every tree, in the which *is* the fruit of a tree yielding seed; to you it shall be for meat.
>
> Genesis 1:29

God clothed Adam and his wife with coats of skins. The coats of skins were probably another type of glory earned for giving name to the living creatures. I do not believe the Lord God killed and skinned animals to make coats for man and woman.

Who needs clothing?

Information about clothing and nakedness can be found elsewhere in the Bible. Believers in Jesus Christ receive seed light or law from the Day of Christ in Heaven. Jesus Christ also urged believers not to be naked or without wedding clothing. In the parable of the marriage feast, we learn the importance of having suitable clothing.

And Jesus answered and spake unto them again by parables, and said,

The kingdom of heaven is like unto a certain king, which made a marriage for his son,

And sent forth his servants to call them that were bidden to the wedding: and they would not come.

Again, he sent forth other servants, saying, Tell them which are bidden, Behold, I have prepared my dinner: my oxen and *my* fatlings *are* killed, and all things *are* ready: come unto the marriage.

But they made light of *it*, and went their ways, one to his farm, another to his merchandise:

And the remnant took his servants, and entreated *them* spitefully, and slew *them*.

But when the king heard *thereof*, he was wroth: and he sent forth his armies, and destroyed those murderers, and burned up their city.

Then saith he to his servants, The wedding is ready, but they which were bidden were not worthy.

Go ye therefore into the highways, and as many as ye shall find, bid to the marriage.

So those servants went out into the highways, and gathered together all as many as they found, both bad and good: and the wedding was furnished with guests.

And when the king came in to see the guests, he saw there a man which had not on a wedding garment:

And he saith unto him, Friend, how camest thou in hither not having a wedding garment? And he was speechless.

Then said the king to the servants, Bind him hand and foot, and take him away, and cast *him* into outer darkness; there shall be weeping and gnashing of teeth.

For many are called, but few *are* chosen.

Matthew 22:1-14

Even though the king called the man friend, the man without the wedding garment was placed into outer darkness. It is a good thing to have the right clothing.

Obeying the light of Jesus Christ is obeying His Word. Those who live their lives in accordance with the Word of God, especially during trials and tribulations, receive an eternal weight of glory.

For our light affliction, which is but for a moment, worketh for us a far more exceeding *and* eternal weight of glory;

II Corinthians 4:17

Eternal weight of glory is the righteousness of God and the clothing needed to stay in the kingdom. In the parable of the wedding feast, if the man had lived his life according to the rules of the kingdom (words from the king), he would have a wedding garment to wear to the feast.

Are we saved by grace?

For by grace are ye saved through faith; and that not of yourselves: *it is* the gift of God:

Not of works, lest any man should boast.

Ephesians 2:8-9

105

By the grace of God we are given a new heart and a new spirit through faith in Jesus Christ. By the grace of God, through faith, the Spirit of God comes and lives within our new spirit.

Our works do not save us, but we do receive an eternal weight of glory by obeying the Word of God and yielding to the Holy Spirit within us.

Is there a Day of Jesus Christ in Heaven?

> His seed also will I make *to endure* for ever, and his throne as the *days* of heaven.
>
> Psalms 89:29
> [*emphasis* added]

This verse is a good place to start in proving the Day of Jesus Christ in Heaven, but we need more evidence.

> And in the days of these kings shall the God of heaven set up a kingdom, which shall never be destroyed: and the kingdom shall not be left to other people, *but* it shall break in pieces and consume all these kingdoms, and it shall stand for ever.
>
> Daniel 2:44

The kingdom in heaven is the same as a creation day in heaven. Light from a creation day is like a kingdom ruling over other kingdoms. There is little or no doubt that these verses refer to Jesus Christ, that same Jesus who shines into His believers' hearts as light from the Day of Jesus Christ in Heaven.

The Fall

Day Six (Day of Man) was created when God spoke the three "Let there be" statements of Day Six concerning man (Genesis 1:26).[12] Day Six was an impersonal universal law like all the creation days before it and it was also an image of God's will.

The man in the Garden of Eden was formed sometime after the seventh day as fruit of Day Six.

Man and woman were naked because there was no seed light going out from Day Six. The Lord God had not judged the first "Let there be" statement of Day Six.

Man was free to eat of every tree in the Garden except the tree of the knowledge of good and evil. That tree was given to Day Five (Creature Day). The fruit on the tree of the knowledge of good and evil was glory earned with the name that Adam gave to the living creatures. That name was the law of man, and Satan was the anointed cherub in charge of administrating that law (Ezekiel 28:14).[13] Satan was also in charge of the fruit on the tree and that is why the serpent could tempt man with the fruit. When Adam gave names to the creatures, he gave the creatures portions of the name Man.

If man ate of the fruit he would leave the Day of Man and die into the Day of Creature.

> But of the tree of the knowledge of good and evil, thou shalt not eat of it: for *in the day* that thou eatest thereof thou shalt surely die.
>
> Genesis 2:17
> [*emphasis* added]

Let's talk about one other tree in the Garden. The tree of life was also there, but it didn't have any fruit on it yet. We can be certain there was no fruit on the tree of life because man would have already eaten from it. After all, he did have permission to eat from every tree in the Garden except for the tree of the knowledge of good and evil. There was no fruit on the tree of the knowledge of good and evil until Adam sowed the law of man to earth's living creatures. There was no fruit on the tree of life until he ate of the tree of the knowledge of good and evil. The eating of the forbidden fruit caused the name Adam to be sowed when God judged living soul man in the Garden. Man left the Garden of Eden as anointed seed light. The anointing on the seed light of man was the name Adam.

Jesus would later humble Himself at God's request and eat of the tree of the knowledge of good and evil. Jesus would die into the day where man went, bringing His anointed light to the hole we fell into. Jesus was anointed with His own name, and after He was baptized, He received His Father's name, which came by the Holy Spirit.

> And lo a voice from heaven, saying, This is my beloved Son, in whom I am well pleased.
>
> Matthew 3:17

Satan was successful by bringing the anointed seed light of man to the Day of the Living Creature.

How did man leave the Garden of Eden?

Every day of creation had an evening and a morning, and sooner or later, each day released a seed light. The seed light of each day would become three forces but remain one seed light. Anointed light from Day Six (Day of Man) also formed three types of spirit forces. Before talking about the three types of spirit forces created by the seed light of man, let's take a look at man when he left Day Six as seed light from that day.

And the Lord God said, Behold, the *man* is become as one of us, to know good and evil: and now, lest *he* put forth *his* hand, and take also of the tree of life, and eat, and live for ever:

Therefore the Lord God sent *him* forth from the garden of Eden, to till the ground from whence *he* was taken.

So he drove out the *man*; and he placed at the east of the garden of Eden Cherubims, and a flaming sword which turned every way, to keep the way of the tree of life.

Genesis 3:22-24

[*emphasis* added]

What happened to Eve?

God mentioned man six times in three verses. Why wasn't woman mentioned even once? Where was she? Remember that man of the Garden was made in the image and the likeness of God. Also, God made man and woman one flesh.

Therefore shall a man leave his father and his mother, and shall cleave unto his wife: and they shall be one flesh.

Genesis 2:24

How could a husband and a wife become one flesh? Weren't they already one flesh or whole? Their bodies were whole, but the flesh God was speaking about was their spiritual flesh or their souls.

And the Lord God caused a deep sleep to fall upon Adam, and he slept: and he took one of his ribs, and closed up the flesh instead thereof;

And the rib, which the Lord God had taken from man, made he a woman, and brought her unto the man.

And Adam said, This *is* now bone of my bones, and flesh of my flesh: she shall be called Woman, because she was taken out of Man.

Genesis 2:21-23

God created woman from a rib He had removed from Adam's body. He did not breath the breath of life into her nostrils like He did with Adam. Adam gave the woman breath of life from his own name when he called her Woman. The name Woman came from the name Man, which is life of the body and is from God and is God.

Please notice that it is written in Genesis 2:23 that woman was created from bone of Adam's bones and flesh of his flesh. God used Adam's rib or bone to create the woman's body. But it was Adam who gave to her of his own flesh, which was life of man and name from the name Man.

Love is the desire to become whole, or one again. Becoming one again with our mate causes our souls to become one again.

Born again Christians receive the name of Jesus in their spirit being, which is Jesus' flesh (John 6:51-58),[14] when they make Jesus their Lord and Savior. The name Jesus becomes their new life. The more Christians become one with Jesus here in the physical world, the more their souls become one or complete in the image of Christ.

Jesus is law of Day Seven. Man left the Garden of Eden as law of Day Six. Jesus came so that man could become images of Him. Living soul man came to give early man the ability to become images of living soul man, which is in the image and the likeness of God the Father, God the Son, and God the Holy Spirit.

When man and woman left the Garden of Eden, they left as one seed light, or the law of man. There was not one law for the creation of man and another one for the creation of woman. They were one species, not two different species. Remember that man and woman were spiritual flesh, not physical flesh.

As mentioned, the seed light of man produced three types of forces. Since the seed light of man was both male and female, so were these three types of forces. When these three spirit forces were activated, they created mind, soul, and heart of man, which are parts of our spirit man or living soul man. Seed light from each of the creation days worked in a similar manner as seed light from Day Six (Day of Man).

Physical Man

What were the jobs of Eve's sons?

We are now able to speak of the three sons of Adam and Eve. Cain was the first born, a tiller of the ground. Abel was next, a keeper of sheep. Physical mothers have physical babies and spiritual mothers have spiritual babies. Eve was of spiritual flesh so her children were spiritual, not physical.

Let's start with Cain. In Genesis it is written that the plants of the field needed a man to till the ground in order that they could grow in the earth.

> And every plant of the field before it was in the earth, and every herb of the field before it grew: for the Lord God had not caused it to rain upon the earth, and *there was* not a man to till the ground.
>
> Genesis 2:5

I believe that the plants of the field were in the earth's spirit world and that the rain that was to come upon the earth was spirit. Remember when Jesus said to the people that His words were spirit and life? Well, the plants were waiting for something similar.

Cain tilled the ground with the rain of spiritual words, not just any words. I believe Cain gave the blessing to the plants that God gave to man for food.

And God blessed them, and God said unto them, Be fruitful, and multiply, and replenish the earth, and subdue it: and have dominion over the fish of the sea, and over the fowl of the air, and over every living thing that moveth upon the earth.

And God said, Behold, I have given you every herb bearing seed, which *is* upon the face of all the earth, and every tree, in the which *is* the fruit of a tree yielding seed; to you it shall be for meat.

And to every beast of the earth, and to every fowl of the air, and to every thing that creepeth upon the earth, wherein *there is* life, I *have given* every green herb for meat: and it was so.

Genesis 1:28-30

The above blessing was the third statement of Day Six concerning man. It was given to man along with the responsibility to give earth's living creatures their food blessing. We can know this because man was to rule over the creatures. In the Bible, blessings and curses are often used to rule.

Abel's power and authority to rule over his sheep came from the second "Let there be" statement of Day Six that gave man dominion over the creatures.

. . . and let them have dominion over the fish of the sea, and over the fowl of the air, and over the cattle, and over all the earth, and over every creeping thing that creepeth upon the earth.

Genesis 1:26

Cain, Abel, and Seth, who were anointed with the name Adam, were seed light from the Day of Man. Each son had his part in the creation of the son-of-man species here upon the physical earth. Cain started the process with the murder of Abel.

> And he said, What has thou done? the voice of thy brother's blood crieth unto me from the ground.
>
> Genesis 4:10

After Cain obeyed Satan and slew Abel, the voice of Abel's blood cried out from the ground to the Lord God. It is written that blood is the life of man (Genesis 9:4).[15]

What was the voice of blood?

Since the voice of Abel came from the blood of Abel, it was a type of spirit or word. Within all humans is the mind, which needs to know God. Could this be the blood of Abel?

The blood of Jesus cleanses us from all unrighteousness and gives us the love for the truth, the truth being God. In a way, the blood of Jesus is crying out to God from believers in the same way as the blood of Abel was crying out to God from Abel's sheep, his believers.

The blood of Abel went into the ground, which was the spirit of his sheep, in order to give them the ability to develop the mind of man. The very same thing happens to believers of Jesus in order for them to develop the mind of Christ.

> And to Jesus the mediator of the new covenant, and to the blood of sprinkling, that speaketh better things than *that of* Abel.
>
> Hebrews 12:24

The mind of Christ, which the blood of Jesus made available, is much better than the mind of man, which the blood of Abel made available.

What was Cain's new job?

When spirit being Seth was born, Eve said that God had given her seed to replace Abel, whom Cain slew (Genesis 4:25).[16] Cain was not Eve's seed even though she gave birth to him. Cain was the seed of the serpent because he yielded to the voice of the serpent in the same way as believers in Jesus Christ are the seed of Abraham through faith (Romans 4:16).[17]

Cain was removed from the presence of God to the spirit side of in the earth. The spirit force of Cain provided the spiritual substance needed to develop souls of man to those who had already developed the mind of man thanks to the blood of Abel.

People formed all kinds of souls. Some had souls to make tents, raise cattle, play musical instruments, and to work with brass and iron.

> And Adah bare Jabal: he was the father of such as dwell in tents, and *of such as have* cattle.
> And his brother's name *was* Jubal: he was the father of all such as handle the harp and organ.
> And Zillah, she also bare Tubalcain, an instructor of every artificer in brass and iron: and the sister of Tubalcain *was* Naamah.
> Genesis 4:20-22

After a soul was developed, name or anointing would flow from the soul to give the maker of the soul the ability to do the things they lusted after.

What did Seth provide?

Abel provided the spiritual substance for mind, and Cain provided the spiritual substance for soul, but there was still something missing. Man needed spiritual substance to develop heart that would be in the presence of God.

Abel's blood went into the ground, and Cain was removed from the presence of God to the spiritual side of the earth.

> And now *art* thou cursed from the earth, which hath opened her mouth to receive thy brother's blood from thy hand;
> When thou tillest the ground, it shall not henceforth yield unto thee her strength; a fugitive and a vagabond shalt thou be in the earth.
> And Cain said unto the Lord, My punishment *is* greater than I can bear.
> Behold, thou hast driven me out this day from the face of the earth; and from thy face shall I be hid; and I shall be a fugitive and a vagabond in the earth; and it shall come to pass, *that* every one that findeth me shall slay me.
> And the Lord said unto him, Therefore whosoever slayeth Cain, vengeance shall be taken on him sevenfold. And the Lord set a mark upon Cain, lest any finding him should kill him.
> And Cain went out from the presence of the Lord, and dwelt in the land of Nod, on the east of Eden.
>
> Genesis 4:11-16

Spirit Adam knew his spirit wife Eve again, and she bore a spirit son whom she named Seth. Seth was to remain in the presence of God. With the birth of Seth, man in the physical world now had the ability to develop the mind, soul, and heart of man. They had the ability to call upon the *name* of the Lord.

> And to Seth, to him also there was born a son; and he called his name Enos: then began men to call upon the name of the Lord.
>
> Genesis 4:26

Seth's ability and authority to provide the substance to create heart came from the first "Let there be" statement of Day Six concerning man and the name Adam.

> And God said, Let us make man in our image, after our likeness...
>
> Genesis 1:26

God used this statement to create man as soul, and then He used the name Adam to make man a living soul. Here in the earth, man's mind, soul, and heart are parts of his spirit man; and our spirit man is living soul man. Those who accept Jesus as Lord and Savior are given a new spirit man, which will at some time in the future lead to the receiving of a new spiritual body.

Who was the first physical Adam?

God answered the first man who called upon Him who had the mind, soul, and heart of a man. God gave him the anointed name of Adam. The anointing or blessing that was the name Adam was then passed down from generation to generation until it was replaced after the Great Flood.

Shortly after the Flood, God gave man another type of dominion over creatures based on fear and dread.

> And God blessed Noah and his sons, and said unto them, Be fruitful, and multiply, and replenish the earth.
>
> And the *fear* of you and the *dread* of you shall be upon every beast of the earth, and upon every fowl of the air, upon all that moveth *upon* the earth, and upon all the fishes of the sea; into your hand are they delivered.
>
> Every moving thing that liveth shall be meat for you; even as the green herb have I given you all things.
>
> Genesis 9:1-3
>
> [*first and second emphasis* added]

Physical Adam gave his blessing to his physical son Seth. Physical Seth was a member of the son-of-man species; whereas, spirit Seth was a member of the man species like Cain, Abel, and living soul man Adam.

How long did it take to become an Adam man?

The process of becoming an Adam man took millions of years. Abel, Cain, and Seth (seed light from Day Six) had a lot of work to do in order to develop man to the point where they could receive the name Adam from God. Adam of the Garden of Eden was the first man to be formed, but he was placed in the Garden of Eden, not here upon the earth.

Physical Adam was not the first man here in the earth but was the first man to receive the name Adam. With the receiving of the name Adam, man had the ability to receive all of the promises that God gave to him and the ability to communicate with God through prayers, obedience, and sacrifices. Man was to be made in God's image and after His likeness, so until early man received the name Adam, in God's eyes they were considered to be less than a man.

What do scientists say about man's development?

Earliest man branched off from ape-like creatures about two million years ago. Our species (Homo sapiens) has been around for 150,000 years. The surprising thing about this is that the brain size of Homo sapiens has not increased in 150,000 years.

In God's eyes, a man was not a man until he had the ability to communicate with God through prayer, obedience, and sacrifices. The man who scientists say evolved two million years ago was only a starting point. Man had to evolve even more to suit God's plan.

How did Homo sapiens evolve?

In the Garden of Eden before the creation of woman, Adam gave name spirit to every living creature so they could develop soul. Adam was a living soul; therefore, that was the type of name spirit he had to give or sow.

Soul name spirit from Adam used the creatures' own mind energies to form souls for the creatures. The soul name spirit they received depended upon the quantity and quality of each creature's mind energies.

After the creatures' souls were formed, desire from the formed souls would control the creatures' minds and bodies.

Because of their behavior over the period of time and generations, their body spirits from the spiritual law substance created on Day Five caused their DNA to change their bodies to suit their behavior. Some of these creatures evolved to become early man.

Man was removed from the Garden and started a family. After Cain murdered his brother Abel, Abel's blood (name spirit) went into the ground (spirits of early man). Early man developed higher minds.

> And Cain talked with Abel his brother: and it came to pass, when they were in the field, that Cain rose up against Abel his brother, and slew him.
>
> And the Lord said unto Cain, Where *is* Abel thy brother? And he said, I know not: *Am* I my brother's keeper?
>
> And he said, What hast thou done? the voice of thy brother's blood crieth unto me from the ground.
>
> And now *art* thou cursed from the earth, which hath opened her mouth to receive thy brother's blood from thy hand;
>
> Genesis 4:8-11

Having received higher minds through the name spirit of Abel, early man made use of fire and tools. Fire was good for keeping predators away at night and for cooking food. Tools were used for protection, hunting, and food preparation.

When early man used fire and tools, their minds received higher energies from their brains. As the result of change in their behavior and their having higher brain energies, spiritual law substance caused their body spirit to change their DNA, which caused their bodies to evolve into the Homo sapien species.

Homo sapiens' higher mind energies were used by man's soul spirit that was received from Cain to form souls of man for Homo sapiens. After souls were formed, desire and lust controlled the minds and bodies of Homo sapiens to receive what they desired or lusted after. As a result of the work of the soul, even higher energies formed in the minds and souls of Homo sapiens.

Man's heart spirit that was received from Seth, who was in the presence of the Lord, caused Homo sapiens to form man hearts. The power of God in the form of the name spirit Adam flowed through the hearts of Homo sapiens. Those who received the name spirit Adam became the son-of-man species.

What was physical Adam?

Physical Adam was the first of the Homo sapiens to receive from God the name spirit called Adam. There were two Adams. First there was the spirit being Adam of the Garden of Eden, and then there were the first Homo sapiens to receive the name Adam.

Why are there human bone fossils?

If you were to sit down and add up the years since physical Adam was here upon the earth, you would come up with a figure close to 6,000 years. This would mean the birth of Adam was around 4005 BC.

Physical Adam walked on earth some 6,000 years ago. He was the first physical man in God's eyes.

Adam was not the first earthy man to evolve two million years ago. He wasn't even the first Homo sapien to evolve 150,000 years ago. However, he was the first Homo sapien to receive the name spirit Adam to become the first member of the son-of-man species.

So, the reason there are fossilized human bones is simple: Our ancestors have been on earth for millions of years.

Young Adam

Living soul man Adam was removed from the Garden of Eden as seed light from the Day of Man (Day Six) and placed upon the spirits of creatures on the earth. Jesus Christ was also a spirit being before coming to the earth to give seed light (Word) to mankind (Philippians 2:6-7).[18]

Since Jesus was born as a physical baby, does that mean living soul man Adam was also born as a physical baby? That's a good question. Let's try to find an equally good answer.

Jesus chose to be born into the son-of-man species in order to save the lost souls. It was early man (evolved creatures) that chose to obey the spirit of man's mind, soul, and then heart to become members of the son-of-man species who God gave the name Adam.

Why was Jesus born?

Why didn't Jesus just offer Himself as spirit to the son-of-man species in order that they could become the son-of-God species? The answer is simple: Jesus had no right to offer the son-of-man species the choice of becoming the son-of-God species. Jesus had to come to this world as a member of the son-of-man species and die on the cross in order to offer His soul as the price for redeeming mankind from Satan.

> Yet it pleased the Lord to bruise him; he hath put *him* to grief: when thou shalt make *his soul an offering for sin*, he shall see *his* seed, he shall prolong *his* days, and the pleasure of the Lord shall prosper in his hand.
>
> Isaiah 53:10
> [*second emphasis* added]

Satan purchased mankind with the fruit on the tree of the knowledge of good and evil. Satan had every legal right to offer seed light from Day Six (Day of Man) to early man of the earth's living-creatures species in order for the creatures to become the son-of-man species. Because of Jesus' death on the cross, Jesus could now offer the son-of-man species an opportunity to become members of the son-of-God species.

Why did God wait so long for Jesus to be born on earth?

Was time needed to prepare a people suitable for the Son of God to be born into? It seems that "yes" would be a reasonable answer.

God gave covenants to Abraham and his seed to prepare a chosen people to receive His Son in the flesh. Each of these covenants came with an anointed name spirit to enforce the blessings and curses connected to each covenant.

Anointed name spirits (angels) have always enforced the covenants of God. God gave the people of Israel another angel when He made the covenant of the law with them in the desert.

> Behold, I send an Angel before thee, to keep thee in the way, and to bring thee into the place which I have prepared.
> Beware of him, and obey his voice, provoke him not; for he will not pardon your transgressions: for my name *is* in him.
> But if thou shalt indeed obey his voice, and do all that I speak; then I will be an enemy unto thine enemies, and an adversary unto thine adversaries.
>
> Exodus 23:20-22

Way back in the Garden of Eden, living soul man also gave the creatures three types of name spirits in order to prepare a species to receive the law of man. Adam gave these three types of names to cattle, fowl of the air, and beast of the field.

> And Adam gave names to all cattle, and to the fowl of the
> air, and to every beast of the field; but for Adam there was not
> found an help meet for him.
>
> Genesis 2:20

As the result of receiving name spirit from Adam, early man evolved about two million years ago. Only early man was capable of receiving seed light from the Day of Man. In the same way, only God's chosen people could receive the "Law" of God. The name spirits God had given to the Jewish people prepared them.

If Adam was born into a physical body before Cain, Abel, and Seth had finished their work, he would have been born into a non-Homo sapien body. I don't know what all that would mean, but the thought of Adam becoming a non-Homo sapien instead of a son-of-man species scares me. Maybe they would have been like the Greek gods or weird mythological creatures. I don't know if they were real, but if they were, thank God for the Flood.

Was it even possible for Jesus to have been born to a people other than God's chosen people?

What would have happened if God had placed His Holy seed into a woman's body that was not prepared by the covenants He gave to the Jewish people? The seed would have become corrupt or the woman would have died; therefore, a virgin mother was required. God had to prepare a sinless body for Jesus. Only a willing virgin from His prepared chosen people would suffice.

Since Adam was with sin, maybe he would not have needed to be born as a baby. Maybe he could have just entered into an obedient servant or worshipper. However, mankind still had to evolve physically and spiritually (mind, soul, and heart) because living soul man was anointed with the name Adam, or the presence of God.

What was Adam's age?

Physical Adam lived 930 years.

> And all the days that Adam lived were nine hundred and thirty years: and he died.
>
> Genesis 5:5

As humans, we naturally think of the 930 years of Adam's life in terms of being born as a baby, living his life as an adult, and then dying as an old man, but Adam was not like us because he was created.

> This *is* the book of the generations of Adam. In the day that God created man, in the likeness of God made he him;
>
> Genesis 5:1

Time and age belong to the world we live in. Adam's age started when he became physical and ended when he died. The Bible doesn't say if Adam was born as a baby after he left the Garden of Eden.

Let's go back to the original question I asked. Was living soul man born into the son-of-man species as a baby or just placed within the body of one particular Homo sapien as higher life spirit to that person?

Jesus needed a sin-free body. Adam was already with sin so he didn't need a sin-free body. How likely was it for Adam to be born as a baby when he didn't have to be one?

It is my own personal opinion that when Adam was removed from the Garden of Eden, he was placed upon spiritual earth, or to be precise, the open firmament of heaven. He was placed there as the law of man to early man.

Later, after Abel, Cain, and Seth had helped early man to evolve into Homo sapiens, living soul man Adam and a particular Homo sapien merged to become physical Adam, the first of the son-of-man species.

Why didn't God just manifest physical bodies for Adam and Jesus?

Why couldn't God just manifest physical bodies for Adam and Jesus? He could have. All things are possible with God (Matthew 19:26). God turned Moses' staff into a serpent (Exodus 7:9-10).[19] John the Baptist told the people that God is able to raise children up to Abraham from stones (Matthew 3:9).[20] Angels sometimes manifest in human bodies, such as the one that wrestled with Jacob (Genesis 32:24-30). If God could do all of these others things, He certainly could have manifested a body for Jesus instead of Him being physically born as a baby.

The problem is that Satan had purchased mankind with the fruit that was upon the tree of the knowledge of good and evil. That fruit was the soul of Satan. We know this because Jesus' soul was the price to redeem man (Isaiah 53:10).

Satan wanted the law of man from Day Six of creation to be applied to earth's living creatures, because he wanted a new species to be created from man and earth's living creatures. The son-of-man species was created, and Satan had dominion over them. To redeem mankind back from Satan, Jesus needed to be born into the son-of-man species' soul. Jesus needed a son-of-man species' soul to hide His Son-of God species' soul from Satan. Satan was the first to use the Trojan horse trick, but Jesus did it better.

Part IV

Bible Mysteries

Bible Mysteries

In this chapter, we shall examine Satan's involvement in man's history, the receiving of name from God, and man's spiritual development. The last thing we shall consider is man's future.

Information received from the preceding chapters is the key to understanding each of the Bible mysteries examined in this chapter. In fact, understanding the following Bible mysteries would be impossible without first knowing how God manifested His Creation. Therefore, one should consider the information presented in this chapter as additional evidence to the validity of this hypothesis.

Many readers will wonder how I managed to piece together the scattered clues that form the pictures that I revealed in this section called "Bible Mysteries" and in the entire book.

If I said it was because of my great intellect, I would be lying. God revealed answers to me as I spent many thousands of hours searching the Scriptures for clues.

What are the greater and lesser lights?

Let's look at the method God used when He gave name-spirit covenants to man.

> And God made two great lights; the greater light to rule the day, and the lesser light to rule the night: *he made* the stars also.
>
> Genesis 1:16

God placed these two lights in the firmament of heaven, the place where the Kingdom of Heaven is located. From this location they ruled the day, which is heaven; and the night, which is the physical world.

God lives in the seventh day, which was formed from the light that was created on the first day. Creation days one and seven and God are in a place that is the highest level of creation. That place is the Kingdom of God.

The lowest level of creation where we live was formed by creation days three, five, and six. The Kingdom of Heaven was formed by creation days two and four. The Kingdom of Heaven is located between our world and the Kingdom of God. God rules the Kingdom of Heaven, and the Kingdom of Heaven rules the earth (Hosea 2:21).[21]

In Revelation 22:16 Jesus said He was the bright and morning star.[22] I do not believe He was speaking of physical stars. I think Jesus was saying He was the greater light in the Kingdom of Heaven.

In Revelation 2:26-28, He promised to give overcomers the morning star, which gave them power over the nations. Surely Jesus was speaking of a spiritual power over nations.[23] He was speaking of saints that had finished their tour of duty here in the earth and had previously died.

When Jesus was born He had his very own star.

> Saying, Where is he that is born King of the Jews? for we have seen his star in the east, and are come to worship him.
> Matthew 2:2

Jesus' star stood over Him when He was a young child.

> When they had heard the king, they departed; and, lo, the star, which they saw in the east, went before them, till it came and stood over where the young child was.
> When they saw the star, they rejoiced with exceeding great joy.
> Matthew 2:9-10

Jesus' star seemed to be very different from the ones we see at night. Could His star have been spiritual in nature and only temporarily manifested in the physical world, like angels sometimes do?

In II Peter 1:19 we learn of the day star that will arise in the hearts of believers. Jesus Christ is the day star.

I claim that the greater light is Jesus, but how could that be? Jesus is God. God is Spirit and Light who lives in the Kingdom of God in the light that was created on the first day.

Yes, Jesus is God, Light, and Spirit that lives above the heavens; but yet, God does have a presence in heaven. I believe the greater light is God's presence in heaven. In a way, it is somewhat like the church being the body of Jesus Christ here in the world while He is in heaven.

Again, it is like our bodies being our presence in this world. We are spirit beings but we still need a presence to live in this physical world.

I want to be perfectly clear about Jesus being the greater light in the spiritual heaven. Christians don't worship the sun, the moon, heavenly bodies or the stars. We worship the Father, the Son, and the Holy Spirit. We worship what lasts forever, not temporary things that will perish someday.

Are you uneasy about my saying the greater light is the body of Jesus Christ in heaven? Fair enough. Pray about it; there is no need to rush to a decision. What I have asked you to contemplate is most certainly controversial, but so is the fact that a lot of people do not believe that God visited the earth two thousand years ago in the form of a man.

Where does the lesser light fit in God's plan? She was the help of the greater light, like the woman was the man's help. Most likely, she was created from part of the greater light since woman was created with part of Adam's body.

As mentioned earlier, the lesser light became the wife of Satan after the greater light refused to eat the fruit that was forbidden for them to eat. After being removed from the name Heaven, she became the great whore and the soul city called Babylon, which was located in the name Seas.

Why did God give names?

When God named living soul man with the name Adam it was similar to Adam's naming earth's living creatures. Both events were attempts to find a helpmate.

Was God looking for a helpmate? Yes He was, but not for Himself. God was seeking a helpmate for the greater light, which was the fruit of Day Four.

As mentioned earlier, living soul man was the fruit of Day Six. He was created with the three "Let there be" statements of Day Six that were spoken concerning man.

The greater light was also fruit. He was fruit of Day Four and was created with the three "Let there be" statements of Day Four.

It is written in the Bible that after looking for a helpmate for living soul man but not finding one, God brought the creatures to Adam, and Adam named them (Genesis 2:18-20).[24]

That makes me believe that there was also no helpmate found for the greater light, so the name "Adam" was given to living soul man to give mankind the ability to become suitable as a helpmate for the greater light, the body for God's presence in heaven. After all, the giving of name to earth's living creatures gave the creatures the ability to become early man with the ability to receive seed light from Day Six (Day of Man) so they could become the son-of-man species.

Living soul man and woman were also supposed to have received seed light from Day Four to become images of Day Four, but they ate of the tree of the knowledge of good and evil before the tree of life had a chance to grow fruit. We know this because they would have eaten of the tree of life if there had been any fruit on it since they had permission to eat of it.

The name that Adam gave to the creatures came from the name "Man." As mentioned, it gave the creatures the ability to develop higher souls, which caused them to evolve into early man. We know this because man was a living soul, and that is the law he had to give to others.

God by the way of the greater light gave living soul man the name Adam, which gave living soul man the ability to develop higher heart and evolve into an image of Day Four.

When Adam gave name to the creatures, he was giving them love, which was giving them name. The receiver of love or name has the power and authority to become an image of the giver of name.

Mankind was supposed to become an image of the greater light. The creatures were supposed to become an image of man. The believers of Jesus Christ are given the name spirit of Jesus in order to develop an image of Jesus in their hearts.

Why did God give names? Giving a name to a lower day is to love that day. Love is the giving of one's power and authority in order to empower the receiver of name to become an image of the giver of name. The purpose of becoming an image is to become a helpmate for companionship.

An example of giving name to receive companionship is when Jesus gave His name to His believers, which is when they receive a new spirit and heart. Believers are formed into an image of Jesus for the purpose of becoming Jesus' companions in heaven some day. While looking for the day they will join Jesus in heaven, believers are busy obeying Jesus and giving Him glory.

Why did the dragon in the Book of Revelation have seven heads?

> And there appeared another wonder in heaven: and behold a great red dragon, having seven heads and ten horns, and seven crowns upon his heads,
>
> Revelation 12:3

Satan became the lesser light's new husband; that is, he ruled over her when she ate of the fruit, which the greater and lesser lights were forbidden to eat. This fruit was created when men knitted their souls and hearts together while building a city and a tower that could reach to heaven.

The lesser light's first husband refused to eat the forbidden fruit on the tree of life. He was allowed to stay in the Garden where God had placed the two of them, but the lesser light was removed.

The Garden where the greater and lesser lights were in was located in the name Heaven; whereas, Adam and Eve were in the Garden within the name Earth. We know this because three "Let there be" statements in the name Heaven created Day Four's "lights in the firmament of heaven," and another three "Let there be" statements in the name Earth created man of Day Six. Man was created to rule over the earth and creatures; whereas, the lights in the firmament of heaven were created to rule over heaven and the earth.

Satan received a new spirit head every time God gave the sons of man a new covenant because he had dominion over man. Each spirit head, or name covenant, was the spiritual power and authority behind one of the seven great worldly kingdoms. Through searching the Scriptures and history, I found the names of the seven heads. The names of the beast's seven spirit heads were Babel, Egypt, Assyria, Babylon, Persia, Greece, and Rome.

The seven names did not stay in the same order as they were given. The second name "Egypt" was removed from the list when its head was wounded to death. Death to a head or name covenant meant that people could no longer receive power and authority when they obeyed the law of that covenant. Death occurred when Egyptian soldiers were drowned in the sea after Israel had passed through on dry land (Isaiah 51:9-10).[25]

The name "Rome" would have been the seventh name, but with the removal of the name "Egypt," Rome became sixth on the list. In Revelation 17:10, Rome is the king that "is." Egypt became the king "who had not yet come," which made it the seventh head.

> And there are seven kings: five are fallen, and one is, *and*
> the other is not yet come; and when he cometh, he must
> continue a short space.
>
> Revelation 17:10

The Egyptian head died in the sea at the time of the Exodus and was removed from the sons of man. This same head became alive; that is, it became available once more to be used by the sons-of-man species when the red dragon was removed from heaven (Revelation 12:7-9).

You may be wondering how the "king who had not yet come" in Revelation 17:10 could have been the Egyptian head that had already come and had already died. When the Egyptian name covenant was alive the first time; that is, it was available to the people, it existed in the spiritual place called the Seas. The seas were created when God gave the name Seas to gathered waters. The Egyptian head or name covenant will be coming to the earth's spiritual realm that was created when God gave the name Earth to dry *land.*

Why are there similarities between the names God gave to people and the names He gave to nations?

By the way of the lesser light, names from God gave those who received these names the ability and authority to rule over nations. Since they came from God in the seventh day, there were seven of them: Babel, Egypt, Assyria, Babylon, Persia, Greece, and Rome.

God by the way of the greater light also gave man seven more name-spirit covenants. Adam was the first name covenant given to man; Noah was the next; then Abraham, Israel, Moses, and David; and then the name covenant that Israel received after the Babylon captivity followed after that.

Since half of the names came by the way of the greater light and half by the way of the lesser light, I believe all fourteen names were really only seven names that were divided into right- and left-hand names.

After the judgment in the Garden of Eden, Adam gave the woman the name Eve. It seems likely to me that after the Tower of Babel event, the greater light also gave name to the lesser light. Why else would both sets of names have seven names each? We also know that the sixth name on each list was given something special. David was given a kingdom, and Greece was given a dominion (II Samuel 2:4 and Daniel 7:6).[26]

Readers who really know the Bible might wonder why the name Isaac was not on the list of seven names. Isaac was left off the list for the same reason Solomon was left off the list. Isaac and Solomon did not receive new covenants from God. They received their father's covenants.

It is written in Revelation 3:1 that after Jesus' death on the cross He had all seven Spirits of God.[27] This was after He defeated Satan and received a name higher than any other name that was mentioned (Philippians 2:9-10).[28] Since Jesus didn't mention the seven names from the greater light and the seven names from the lesser light, it seems reasonable to believe that both sets of names together were really only one set of name Spirits from God that was divided.

> And the seventh angel sounded; and there were great voices in heaven, saying, The kingdoms of this world are become *the kingdoms* of the Lord, and of his Christ; and he shall reign for ever and ever.
>
> Revelation 11:15

The lesser light is the great whore and ruler of the mighty soul city of Babylon, within the name Seas. We learn by reading the Book of Revelation that she will lose her power over the nation and it will be given to Jesus' new bride, the church or dead saints.

Jesus will keep His promise to the overcomers and give them power over the nations (Revelation 2:26). This will be accomplished when He gives them the morning star (Revelation 2:28).

In the Book of Revelation, why do the numbers 666 represent the antichrist?

No other number in history has captivated man like the number 666. Just hearing or seeing the number 666 causes many people to fear, but why does the number 666 represent the antichrist, which is the beast out of the earth?

> And that no man might buy or sell, save he that had the mark, or the name of the beast, or the number of his name.
> Here is wisdom. Let him that hath understanding count the number of the beast: for it is the number of a man; and his number *is* Six hundred threescore *and* six.
>
> Revelation 13:17-18

The number 666 is the number of the beast's name, and the beast is a man. The dragon gave the beast his power, his seat, and great authority.

> And the beast which I saw was like unto a leopard, and his feet were as *the feet* of a bear, and his mouth as the mouth of a lion: and the dragon gave him his power, and his seat, and great authority.
>
> Revelation 13:2

Since Satan is the source of all that the beast is, I believe that the beast is just another form of Satan in the same way that Jesus and the Holy Spirit are forms of the Father God.

God reminded Satan that he was a man and not a God.

> Son of man, say unto the prince of Tyrus, Thus saith the Lord God; Because thine heart is lifted up, and thou hast said, I am a God, I sit in the seat of God, in the midst of the seas; yet thou art a man, and not God, though thou set thine heart as the heart of God:
>
> Ezekiel 28:2

After reading Revelation 13:17-18 and Ezekiel 28:2, we know four things. Satan has a name, the number of his name is 666, the number of Satan's name is a number of a man, and finally, Satan is a man.

Why would the number 666 be a number of a man? I can think of only one reason. Man was created with three "Let there be" statements spoken on Day Six concerning man. It seems reasonable to believe that the number 666 represents the three "Let there be" statements spoken on Day Six of creation concerning man. Since the three "Let there be" statements that were spoken on Day Six created man, the name "man" also represents the three statements spoken by God on Day Six.

Why would Satan's name be the three "Let there be" statements spoken on Day Six? We are shown in the following verse that Satan was an anointed cherub who covereth.

> Thou art the anointed cherub that covereth: and I have set thee so: thou wast upon the holy mountain of God: thou hast walked up and down in the midst of the stones of fire.
>
> Ezekiel 28:14

What did Satan seek to gain? In Ezekiel 28:2 we learn that Satan wanted to be a God.

God rules over His spoken Word, and His Word rules over all His Creation. Satan wanted to rule over God's spoken Word.

We learn in the following verses that Satan's ultimate goal was to rule over the stars of God, which I believe are the greater light and lesser light. His first goal was to rule over God's spoken words that created man in order to rule over man. He wanted to rule over the three "Let there be" statements spoken on Day Six, which created man.

> How art thou fallen from heaven, O Lucifer, son of the morning! how art thou cut down to the ground, which didst weaken the nations! For thou hast said in thine heart, I will

ascend into heaven, I will exalt my throne above the stars of God: I will sit also upon the mount of the congregation, in the sides of the north: I will ascend above the heights of the clouds; I will be like the most High.

Isaiah 14:12-14

The number 666 represents the three "Let there be" statements that created man. For Satan to become master over Day Six, or the Day of Man, he needed victories over each of the three "Let there be" statements of that day.

Satan's first victory came when he got both the man and the woman in the Garden of Eden to eat of the forbidden fruit. Satan's second victory came when he was able to persuade Cain to kill Abel. His third victory was accomplished when he convinced man to knit their hearts and souls together by building a city and a tower to reach unto heaven in order for them to make a name for themselves. Satan would receive authority over any name they received because he had dominion over man.

How did Satan become the ruler over the three "Let there be" statements of Day Six concerning man?

The first "Let there be" statement of Day Six created man in the image and in the likeness of God; that is, man was created a living soul. Adam gave name to earth's living creatures. Adam was a living soul; therefore, the name he gave to the creatures was for the making of souls. This was the first "Let there be" statement of Day Six concerning man.

Adam had ruled over the name he spoke to the creatures. Satan was an anointed cherub that covereth (Ezekiel 28:14). Satan's job was to enforce the blessings and curses in regards to the covenant name Adam spoke to the creatures. All covenant names have blessings and curses, which are enforced by angels. Earth's living creatures were successful in forming souls, which they needed for evolving. Satan earned glory for his work. Satan's glory was the fruit on the tree of the knowledge of good and evil. Satan's glory was also his soul. We know this because Jesus' soul was the price needed to redeem mankind back from Satan.

> Yet it pleased the Lord to bruise him; he hath put him to grief: when thou shalt make his soul an offering for sin, he shall see his seed, he shall prolong his days, and the pleasure of the Lord shall prosper in his hand.

> Isaiah 53:10

When man and woman ate of the forbidden fruit, Satan became the ruler over the first "Let there be" statement of Day Six, and man was removed from the Garden.

When man was in the Garden, he was protected and provided for by God. God gave them every tree in the Garden to eat except the tree of the knowledge of good and evil. God protected man by telling them the truth about that tree. He told both the man and the woman that if they ate of the tree of the knowledge of good and evil that they would die from the Day of Man into the Day of the Creature. We can know this because God told the man that he would die in the day that he ate of the forbidden fruit. Since man did not die physically, we know he died spiritually. Man lost his home in the spiritual place that was the Garden of Eden. Today man's home is in the physical bodies created under the law of creatures on Day Five.

Satan's second victory came when he persuaded Cain to kill Abel. Before his death, Abel used the authority of the second "Let there be" statement spoken on Day Six concerning man to have dominion over the earth's living creatures, which were called sheep. When Abel's blood went into the ground, Satan became the ruler of the second "Let there be" statement of Day Six. At that time, the number of his name was 66.

Cain became Satan's seed like those who have faith in Jesus become the seed of Abraham (I John 3:12 and Romans 4:13-16).[29] Satan needed his seed to grow and spread in order to have enough workers to accomplish his last victory.

Cain was a tiller of the ground. He received his authority from the third "Let there be" statement concerning man, which is found in Genesis 1:27-30. The words "Let there be" are not actually written in the Bible concerning the food blessing from God to man and creatures, but when we compare Genesis 1:22, a blessing for the creatures on Day Five, to what is written in Genesis 1:27-30, it is clear that this statement is also a "Let there be" statement.

Satan received the last six in the number of his name at the Tower of Babel. He convinced the people to build a city and a tower to reach into heaven in order for them to make a name for themselves. In doing so, they knitted their hearts and souls together and created glory for their ruler "Satan."

The people's souls were created with law from Day Six, the Day of Man. We know this because man was a living soul.

Their hearts were created with the name "Adam." Jesus was the last Adam (I Corinthians 15:45).[30] When believers accept Jesus as Lord and Savior, they are given a new spirit and a new heart. That makes me believe that the name Adam was used to develop higher hearts.

Day Six (man) was the seed that created the tree of the knowledge of good and evil. Day Four (lights in the firmament) was the seed that created the tree of life.

When the people built a city and a tower, they created two types of glory: soul and heart.

On the cross Jesus covered up his Son-of-God soul with His Son-of-Man soul to fool Satan into accepting Him into Hell? Satan did the same thing upon the tree of life at the time of the Tower of Babel. Earlier in history, Satan covered the glory earned by obeying law of Day Five, with glory earned by obeying name from Adam in order to tempt man and woman in the Garden of Eden. The fruit on the tree of the knowledge of good and evil and the fruit on the tree of life were good to look at but deadly inside if you were not supposed to eat of them.

Why were earth's living creatures created on Day Six?

In Genesis 1:24-25, God spoke the "Let there be" statement that created living creatures. Even though God spoke this statement on the sixth day, the "Let there be" statement that created living creatures belonged to Day Five. As we learned earlier, creation days were God's creations, not periods of time.

God waited until the sixth day to speak the third "Let there be" statement of Day Five because He needed man to give the creatures names, which they used to form souls.

Since today man exists here in the physical world within a living creature's body, God must have spoken the third "Let there be" statement of Day Five on Day Six because He knew man would die into the fifth day and become physical beings here in the earth.

Who was Satan trying to tempt at the Tower of Babel?

Satan was trying to tempt the greater light and his helpmate the lesser light. They were the fruit of Day Four.

When man received the name Adam, he gave part of the name Man to earth's living creatures. When the greater light received name from God, he too gave part of his name to a lower day. Man was that lower day, and Adam was the name, which came from God by the way of the greater light.

The first to be tempted by the fruit on the tree of life, which was forbidden to them just like the fruit on the tree of the knowledge of good and evil was forbidden to man, was the lesser light. She was the helpmate of the greater light. Unlike the man Adam, the greater light refused to eat of the forbidden fruit. We can know the greater light refused because he was not removed from heaven.

When woman had eaten of the forbidden fruit, Adam named her Eve, which came from his name. The greater light gave the lesser light part of his name when she had eaten of the fruit that was forbidden to them. That name was Babel and she became the great whore. God removed her from her husband and gave her to the son-of-man species as name spirit, which Satan had dominion over.

Through the years by the way of the lesser light, God would issue a total of seven name covenants to the son-of-man species. The names Babel, Egypt, Assyria, Babylon, Persia, Greece, and Rome were used to rule seven worldly nations and to receive glory and riches for the lesser light and her new husband (Satan).

By the way of the greater light God also gave seven name spirits to the son-of-man species. The name Adam was replaced at the time of the Flood. After that, man then received the following name covenants: Noah, Abraham, Israel, Moses, David, and the covenant that Israel received after they returned from Babylon.

God's purpose for giving name covenants by the way of the greater light was to prepare a people for the coming of Jesus, His Christ, and to receive glory and riches for the greater light (Jesus). The purpose for giving name by the lesser light was to prepare the way of the antichrist.

Today, the Spirit of God and the spirit of the antichrist are at war in the minds and hearts of mankind. They are fighting for souls and the right to mark their followers with either the mark of God or the mark of the antichrist.

Why are there similarities between Jesus as name covenant and the great red dragon, Jesus in the flesh and the beast out of the sea, and the Holy Spirit and the beast out of the earth?

Before Jesus came in the flesh, he was removed from heaven and given to Israel as a name-spirit covenant, after the captivity in Babylon.

> I the Lord have called thee in righteousness, and will hold thine hand, and will keep thee, and give thee for a covenant of the people, for a light of the Gentiles;
>
> Isaiah 42:6

Satan, as the red dragon, was removed from heaven as name spirit.

And the great dragon was cast out, that old serpent, called the Devil, and Satan, which deceiveth the whole world: he was cast out into the earth, and his angels were cast out with him.

Revelation 12:9

Jesus was manifested in the flesh. He preached three and one-half years to the Jewish people to whom He was sent. Jesus had power over all demons. He also said in Revelation 3:1 that He had the seven Spirits of God.

Jesus died on the cross to offer His soul as the price to buy back man from Satan (Isaiah 53:10).

Jesus obeyed His Father and received His power from His Father. He preached repentance from sin and obedience to the Father. Only those who the Father had given to Him could receive Jesus (John 6:65).[31]

Jesus was wounded to death and was in the ground for three days before He rose again. Jesus was the Lamb of God.

The beast that rose up out of the sea had seven heads. One of the seven heads was wounded to death and lived again. He received the power, seat, and authority from the dragon (Revelation 13:1-4).

The beast out of the sea preached blasphemy three and one-half years against God and was given power over the saints to overcome them. Those not written in the book of life of the Lamb had to worship him (Revelation 13:5-8).

Jesus, as name covenant, and Satan, as name spirit, are opposite of each other as well as Jesus in the flesh and the beast out of the sea are opposite of each other. Yet somehow they seem to be the same in many ways.

What do the Holy Spirit and the antichrist have in common?

The Holy Spirit came from heaven in the form of a cloven tongue like as of fire and He only spoke the words He heard the Father and the Son speak.

The beast out of the earth, which is the spirit of the antichrist, had two horns like a lamb and spoke like his father, the dragon (Revelation 13:11).

Believers of Jesus Christ can do miracles through the Holy Spirit and in the name of Jesus. The beast out of the earth can also do miracles in the sight of the first beast (Revelation 13:14).

The Holy Spirit encourages believers to obey the Word of God, which causes Christ to form in their new hearts as an image of Jesus. The beast causes people to make an image of the first beast (Revelation 13:14).

The Holy Spirit has the power to give life to the Word of God that has formed in the hearts of believers. Life in the Word spoken from the hearts of believers can cause others to believe in Jesus Christ. This life-filled Word causes believers to put the desire of their old sinful nature to death. The beast out of the earth has power to give life to the image of the first beast, which gives it the ability to speak and cause people who will not worship the image of the beast to be killed (Revelation 13:15).

The Holy Spirit seals believers with the mark of God, which is the number of the name of God, the name of the city of God, and the name of Jesus' new name. The number of all three of these names is 777. Without this mark, no one can enter the New Jerusalem (Revelation 22:3-4). The beast out of the earth causes people to receive the mark of the beast or the number of his name, which is 666. Without this mark no one can buy or sell. At the final judgment, those with the mark of the beast will be placed into the "lake of fire" (Revelation 19:20).

Why are there so many similarities between Jesus as name covenant and the great red dragon, Jesus in the flesh and the beast out of the sea, and the Holy Spirit and the beast out of the earth (antichrist)? What could they possibly have in common?

Jesus as name covenant, Jesus in the flesh, and the Holy Spirit are all forms of Jesus as name covenant, which is a form of God the Father. The great red dragon, the beast out of the sea, and the beast out of the earth are all forms of the great red dragon, which is a form of Satan.

Jesus ruled over the seven name covenants from God by the way of the greater light. Satan ruled over the seven name covenants from God by the way of the lesser light. Both sets of name covenants came from one name that was given to the greater light, which was divided at the time of the Tower of Babel, hence the similarities between Jesus and his different forms and Satan and his different forms.

Who were the ten-toe kingdoms?

It is written in the Book of Daniel that King Nebuchadnezzar dreamt about an image. The image's head was made of gold, his breast and arms were made of silver, his belly and thighs were made of brass, his legs were made of iron, and his feet were made of part iron and part clay. It is easy to understand from reading the Bible that gold represented Babylon, silver represented Persia, brass represented Greece, and iron represented Rome. The identifications of the iron and clay nations were not revealed. People have been wondering about the ten-toe kingdoms ever since that time.

These very same ten-toe kingdoms can be found in the Book of Revelation. It is written in the following verse that the beast, which the great whore sat on, had ten horns.

So he carried me away in the spirit into the wilderness: and I saw a woman sit upon a scarlet colored beast, full of names of blasphemy, having seven heads and ten horns.

Revelation 17:3

In the following verse the ten horns are identified as ten kings who had yet to receive their kingdoms.

> And the ten horns which thou sawest are ten kings, which have received no kingdom as yet; but receive power as kings one hour with the beast.
>
> Revelation 17:12

Jesus Christ came in the flesh to offer His soul for our sins, but that was only part of the reason He came. Jesus came in the flesh to create the fruit for an offering. Jesus had the seven Spirits of God. By living in the flesh and obeying all seven name Spirits of God, He created fruit acceptable to be offered to God.

Jesus' fruit was accepted and as a result of this, the seven Spirits of His church within the Holy Spirit were made available to His believers. Believers must overcome each one by obeying each Spirit and developing the fruit that is acceptable. There were seven different rewards promised to the overcomers (Revelation 2 & 3).

One might say okay, but what does this have to do with the ten-toe kingdoms? Please read the following Bible verse.

> And there appeared another wonder in heaven; and behold a great red dragon, having seven heads and ten horns, and seven crowns upon his heads.
>
> Revelation 12:3

Please notice two things about this verse. First, the dragon had seven crowns to match his seven heads. Secondly, he did not have any crowns to match his ten horns.

Crowns are statements of victory. Satan had already developed the fruit to receive the crowns for the seven heads, which I believe were the name spirits of Babel, Egypt, Assyria, Babylon, Persia, Greece, and Rome.

Because of the victories represented by the seven crowns on the seven heads, the beast out of the sea made seven name spirits available for the creation of worldly nations. Any nation that obeyed one or more of these seven name spirits would receive power to create a worldly nation. This power to create nations comes in the form of emotional power over people, which blind them from the truth.

Have you ever wondered how leaders like Hitler could get so many good people to do evil? The answer lies in the fact that the leaders themselves first became servants of a ten-toe kingdom and slaves to their own evil thoughts and dark emotions. Ten-toe kingdom leaders are very believable because they are convinced that their ways are right.

When the dragon was removed from heaven, he persecuted the woman.

> And when the dragon saw that he was cast unto the earth,
> he persecuted the woman which brought forth the man child.
>
> Revelation 12:13

He unleashed seven evil-nation spirits upon the woman who brought forth the man-child, who was Jesus. The woman was the Jewish nation.

We know the dragon had seven name spirits available because he had seven crowns upon his seven heads, which were seven name spirits to create nations. The ten horns that the dragon had were also types of name spirits. They were ten chances for someone to become a king.

To become a king, a person had to develop the fruit that would be acceptable. Ten evil people had a chance to become a king under Satan. Each of the ten "would-be kings" had to be extremely evil in a certain area. For example, Hitler had powerful fruit in the area of hating Jews. If he had lived at the right time, he might have become the king of hate.

Kings of the ten-toe kingdoms would have to wait until the beast out of the sea came on the scene before they received their kingdoms.

And I stood upon the sand of the sea, and saw a beast rise up out of the sea, having seven heads and ten horns, and upon his horns ten crowns, and upon his heads the name of blasphemy.

Revelation 13:1

The ten crowns upon his ten horns indicate that he had received victory in ten areas. Ten evil spirits became available to anyone who obeyed them, rather they knew it or not. The ten-toe-kingdom kings were the rulers over these spirits and anyone who obeyed any of the ten evil spirits. Kingdoms in the spiritual world rule kingdoms here in the physical world.

Many people believe that the ten-toe kingdoms are ten worldly nations, but there are two things wrong with this way of thinking. Since the ten-toe kingdoms have a spiritual base, there can be any number of them here in the earth over time, and they don't have to be nations. The ten-toe kingdoms can be a single person or a single nation, and any kind of organization in between. One only needs to obey one or more of the ten-toe kings of the spirit world to receive power from them.

A ten-toe kingdom can be recognized by their emotional power over people. Emotional power can be transferred to things like selling power, celebrity power, pride, votes for a certain party or cause, nationalism, and rationalism to mention a few.

The emotional power of the ten-toe kingdoms is hidden from its subjects. Neither the leaders nor the members of the ten-toe kingdoms know they are being controlled. When people obey the emotional power of the ten-toe kingdoms, they actually think that they are obeying their own will. They say things like "It's my body, it's my money, it's my company, and I will do what I want to do." So many people are being controlled and they don't even know it.

Those who think they are doing their own will, but are really being controlled by the ten-toe kingdoms and the antichrist, will be marked with the number 666 and they won't even know it. The antichrist's number will be placed on their spirit man, not their physical bodies. It is the spirit man that will be going into the lake of fire, not the physical bodies. The ten-toe kingdoms are to Satan what the church is to Jesus. One has to choose to be in Jesus' church. In Satan's church many of his congregation doesn't even know that they are members.

The doors to Satan's church are open wide. We are all tempted at times to yield to evil emotions and evil desires, such as hate, jealously, envy, adultery, idolatry, lust, and unforgiveness. If we don't ask God to forgive our sins and to give us another spirit and another heart, the number 666 will be placed on our spirit man.

I have heard many people say they would choose death before they would let the antichrist mark them with the number 666. Little do these people know that every time they yield to an evil emotion or an evil desire, they are coming closer to receiving the mark of the antichrist and becoming a subject of the ten-toe kingdoms.

Those who are marked with the number 666 are given the ability to buy and to sell (Revelation 13:17). Buying and selling is the receiving of power from Satan and the giving of power from Satan to others.

Christians who are marked with God's number can also receive and give or transfer the power of God to other believers by laying-on of hands. This makes the anointing of God available, which is the power of God to do His will.

Where does the beast out of the earth fit into Satan's evil plan?

The last beast is the antichrist. His job is the same as the Holy Spirit, but the opposite. He encourages evil doing and rebellion against God. He also gives power to those who have created evil images of the first beast in their heart. He gave them power to overcome the good that is in them in order to do evil.

And he had power to give life unto the image of the beast, that the image of the beast should both speak, and cause that as many as would not worship the image of the beast should be killed.

Revelation 13:15

If one doesn't have the mark of God and the seal of salvation, they are targets and fair game to evil spirits. Whenever anyone looks upon, thinks about, or imagines doing evil, they are obeying an evil spirit, which causes them to develop fruit. When their fruit is accepted, they will be given the power to overcome any good that is in them. For anyone to do evil to others, they must first overcome the good that is in them. For anyone to do good for others, they must first overcome the evil that is in them.

The image of the beast that is in the hearts of those who obey the antichrist is the fruit that overcomes any good they may have in them. The image of Jesus that forms in the hearts of His believers is the fruit that overcomes any evil they may have in them.

Ever since I was a little boy I have been warned about the coming of the antichrist. No one warned me that he was already here in the earth and available to anyone who will listen to him. If I had read the Bible, I could have seen for myself that the spirit of the antichrist was already in the earth.

Little children, it is the last time: and as ye have heard that anti-christ shall come, even now are there many anti-christs; whereby we know that it is the last time.

I John 2:18

If the antichrist came in a physical body he could only be one place at a time, but by coming in the form of a name spirit, the beast out of the earth can be everywhere and do billions of times more damage than one lonely beast.

That is why Jesus said it was better for the people if He would go away and He would send back a Comforter, which means the Holy Spirit (John 16:7).[32] The Comforter can be everywhere at the same time.

As part of the judgment in the Garden of Eden, Satan was told he would crawl on his belly all the days of his life (Genesis 3:14).[33] Where is it written that Satan's sins were forgiven? There is no place written in the Bible that says Satan's sins were forgiven and that he can once more walk upon his legs.

Since the dragon, the beast out of the sea, and the beast out of the earth are three forms of the being called Satan, I don't think anyone of them will have legs here in the physical world; or in other words, they won't have physical bodies.

Knowing this, you should make sure you know what kind of music your children are listening to and what kind of movies they are watching. Don't wait until their fruit has been picked to find out.

Be sober, be vigilant; because your adversary the devil, as a roaring lion, walketh about, seeking whom he may devour:

I Peter 5:8

Why are some people seriously affected when exposed to sexual and violent stimuli and others seem to suffer little or no bad effects? There seems to be at least three major factors which determine who will imitate what they see and hear.

The state of mind of the one exposed to sex and violence contributes to how they process such information. Obviously, a well-adjusted individual has a greater chance of not being adversely affected by what they are exposed to than a less stable person who is perhaps suffering from some kind of stress or pain.

The amount of exposure to sex and violence is another major factor in determining if an individual will be unfavorably affected by exposure to improper stimuli. It is obvious that the more one sees or hears something the more chances they will have to be affected by what they are seeing and hearing.

Lastly, it is the individual that determines the effect sex and violence will have on them. We as individuals choose the amount and the kind of emotion we apply to unhealthy stimuli. We also choose the amount of times we are exposed to such stimuli.

If a person finds oneself desiring to experience more and more unhealthy stimuli, that person is in real trouble. That person must find a way to stop feeding evil spirits. Before one can stop doing a bad habit, one must stop thinking about it and replace the bad thoughts with good thoughts. Seeking advice from a good church could help.

To the individual who finds oneself in the above situation, I have two suggestions. First that individual should be afraid, very afraid. Secondly, that individual should ask Jesus Christ to save him/her.

What were the sea and the earth from which the beasts rose out of?

Have you ever considered that the sea and the earth where the two beasts rose out of could have been something other than H_2O oceans and the earth we stand upon? There are other options to consider.

Some time ago, I mentioned my belief that the names of Day, Night, Heaven, Seas, and Earth were name spirits from God and places where spirit beings exist. The name Earth was given to dry *land* and is the spiritual heart of all physical matter, including our planet Earth. The name Seas was given to the gathering of the waters on Day Three. Seas is the soul of the earth and is attached to the nonmass energies of this universe, including those associated with our planet.

The name spirits of Adam, Noah, Abraham, Israel, Moses, and David exist in the heart of the earth, which is the name Earth. The name spirits of Babel, Egypt, Assyria, Babylon, Persia, Greece, and Rome exist in the soul of the earth, which is the name Seas.

Did you notice that I did not mention the name Jesus when I was naming those of the heart of the earth? Because of the work Jesus completed on the cross, Jesus' followers will be going to His bosom in Heaven, not the heart of the earth.

We are confident, I say, and willing rather to be absent from the body, and to be present with the Lord.

II Corinthians 5:8

When the red dragon was removed from heaven, I hypothesized that he went into the soul of the name Rome. Rome's soul was in the name Seas. From this location, the red dragon sent forth the beast out of the seas as a spirit being to preach blasphemies to the dead in the heart of the earth for three and one-half years. The heart of the earth is within the name of the Earth.

And there was given unto him a mouth speaking great things and blasphemies; and power was given unto him to continue forty *and* two months.

Revelation 13:5

The second beast came forth out of the heart of the earth. He does the same job for the beast out of the sea as the Holy Spirit does for Jesus. The beast out of the earth encourages people to obey the beast out of the sea. The Holy Spirit encourages people to obey Jesus. The beast that rose out of the sea, and the beast that rose out of the earth were both forms of Satan, like Jesus and the Holy Spirit are forms of the Father. Both beasts were spirit beings that came out of the earth's spirit realms.

Will our planet and our universe be destroyed?

And I saw a new heaven and a new earth: for the first heaven and the first earth were passed away; and there was no more sea.

Revelation 21:1

It is clearly stated in Revelation 21:1 that heaven and the earth had passed away, and there was no more sea. But could the heaven, the earth, and the sea that's written about in Revelation 21:1 be of a

spiritual nature instead of a physical nature? Whenever there is a question about the meaning of the written Word, we are to let the Scriptures interpret the Scriptures. That is, we are to search the Scriptures for understandings.

> And there was war in heaven: Michael and his angels fought against the dragon; and the dragon fought and his angels,
> And prevailed not; neither was their place found any more in heaven.
> And the great dragon was cast out, that old serpent, called the Devil, and Satan, which deceiveth the whole world: he was cast out into the earth, and his angels were cast out with him.
>
> Revelation 12:7-9

There are two very important points to consider about this great event in history. When Satan as the great red dragon was removed from heaven, even the place where he existed at in heaven was also done away with. This is a clue to why God saw fit to remove the old earth and the sea.

Apparently, whenever and wherever God removes evil spirits, He also removes the places where they exist. That makes me wonder how much damage evil spirits can do to their surroundings.

The second point we need to consider is that Satan as the great red dragon and his angels are spirit beings. They don't have physical bodies. They only have spiritual bodies; therefore, when God removed them from heaven He placed them in the earth's spiritual realms. We will return to this point soon.

Let's look at another eviction.

> And the beast was taken, and with him the false prophet that wrought miracles before him, with which he deceived them that had received the mark of the beast, and them that worshipped his image. These both were cast alive into a lake of fire burning with brimstone.
>
> Revelation 19:20

When God removed Satan from heaven, He also removed Satan's place in heaven. Does this mean that when the beast out of the sea and the beast out of the earth, which is the false prophet, are removed from the sea and from the earth that their places will also be removed?

It is confirmed in the following verse that both the old earth and the sea were no more.

> And I saw a new heaven and a new earth: for the first heaven and the first earth were passed away; and there was no more sea.
>
> Revelation 21:1

This verse let's us know that death and hell will also be removed from their usual locations and placed into the lake of fire.

> And death and hell were cast into the lake of fire. This is the second death.
>
> Revelation 20:14

Both death and hell are places where spirits exist. Death is located in the name spirit Seas before being placed in the lake of fire. Hell was located in the name spirit Earth, which is the heart of the earth, before being placed in the lake of fire.

Satan as the great red dragon and his angels are spirit beings. They were removed from a spiritual place called heaven. It only makes sense that they were placed in the earth's spirit realms.

The beast out of the sea and the beast out of the earth (the false prophet) are forms of Satan, just like Jesus and the Holy Spirit are forms of the Father. Since Satan is a spirit being, chances are good that both the beast out of the sea and the beast out of the earth are also spirit beings. They too would exist in spirit realms.

Earth's spirit realms were created when God gave the spirit name Earth to dry *land* and the spirit name Seas to gathered waters (Genesis 1:10). In Revelation 21:1, the heaven and the earth that passed away, and the sea that was no more are all spirit places where Satan and his followers existed before going into the lake of fire.

When someone accepts Jesus Christ as Lord and Savior, they are given a new spirit and a new heart, which is the name spirit of Jesus Christ. They are not given new physical bodies. Sometime in the future, after the loss of their physical bodies, they will receive new spiritual bodies (I Corinthians 15:44).[34]

I suggest to you that heaven's body, the earth's body, and the sea's body may not be destroyed at the time Revelation 21:1 is referring to; but the body of heaven, which is firmament, will receive a new name spirit called the New Heaven. The body of earth, which is dry *land*, will receive a new name spirit called the New Earth. Lastly, the body of the Seas, which is gathered waters, will also receive a new name spirit called Second Death (Revelation 20:12-15).[35]

New name spirits became necessary because the presence of Satan had corrupted their old name spirits. Will our planet and our universe be destroyed? Yes, they certainly will be destroyed. Death of our planet will probably come when our sun expands as it grows old. The planet Earth might even last until the universe ends.

As to when our universe will end, it is when God will speak the three "Let there be" statements that were missing from the first chapter of the Book of Genesis, which are "Let the light be divided from the darkness," which will place all that belongs to God, within God; "Let there be darkness," which will dissolve all spiritual matter into spiritual energy; and "Let there be waters," which will dissolve all matter into energy.

I don't know when or how our planet will end, but I do know that in Revelation 21:1 the first heaven, the first earth, and the sea are spirit places for spirit beings, and they will be replaced with new name spirits.

God destroyed the heavens and the earth at the time of the Flood.

Whereby the world that then was, being overflowed with water, perished:

But the heavens and the earth, which are now, by the same word are kept in store, reserved unto fire against the day of judgment and perdition of ungodly men.

II Peter 3:6-7

The spiritual heavens and the spiritual earth surrounding the physical earth were destroyed at the time of the Flood and were replaced with new spiritual heavens and a new spiritual earth, but the physical heavens and the physical earth remained. It seems reasonable to believe that something similar could happen again in the future.

Why did God punish man and beast with the Flood?

Men on the earth have the bodies of earth's living creatures or beasts. The souls they developed wanted only to satisfy the wants of creatures' bodies. They imagined only evil thoughts in their hearts.

And God saw that the wickedness of man *was* great in the earth, and *that* every imagination of the thoughts of his heart *was* only evil continually.

Genesis 6:5

Men's hearts were in the presence of God. Men on the earth received power from God through their hearts. Men used God's power to do evil. God created the Flood to remove the name Adam, which was a covenant given to man from God, and also part of the name Man, which Adam gave to the creatures.

And it repented the Lord that he had made man on the earth, and it grieved him at his heart.

Genesis 6:6

What were the covenants God gave to man and creatures after the Flood?

God removed the power and authority from the first "Let there be" statement of Day Four and gave the power and authority of the second "Let there be" statement of Day Four to create this karma-like law.

> While the earth remaineth, seedtime and harvest, and cold and heat, and summer and winter, and day and night shall not cease.
>
> Genesis 8:22

Now take a look at the following verse.

> . . .and let them be for signs, and for seasons, and for days, and years:
>
> Genesis 1:14

Can you tell that the covenant found in Genesis 8:22 came from the power and authority of God's spoken words found in Genesis 1:14?

God also removed the power and authority from the first "Let there be" statement concerning man and replaced it with the power and authority of the second "Let there be" statement concerning man's receiving dominion.

> . . .and let them have dominion over the fish of the sea, and over the fowl of the air, and over the cattle, and over all the earth, and over every creeping thing that creepeth upon the earth.
>
> Genesis 1:26

If you were to examine the covenant that God gave to Noah and his sons, you can see it was the dominion covenant of Genesis 1:26.

And God blessed Noah and his sons, and said unto them, Be fruitful, and multiply, and replenish the earth.

And the fear of you and the dread of you shall be upon every beast of the earth, and upon every fowl of the air, upon all that moveth *upon* the earth, and upon all the fishes of the sea; into your hand are they delivered.

Every moving thing that liveth shall be meat for you; even as the green herb have I given you all things.

Genesis 9:1-3

You might be thinking that God had already given this blessing or "Let there be" statement to man. Yes, He did give this blessing to man, but man at that time was only a spirit being or a living soul. Man had now become one with earth's living beasts; that is, man had become earth's living beast's spirit man.

As a side note, at the time of the Tower of Babel, man would receive the third "Let there be" statement of Day Four, which brought light to the earth to give power over nations.

And let them be for lights in the firmament of the heaven to give light upon the earth: and it was so.

Genesis 1:15

Both man and beast also received the last "Let there be" statement of Day Six, which was a blessing from God to provide for food.

And God blessed them, and God said unto them, Be fruitful, and multiply, and replenish the earth, and subdue it: and have dominion over the fish of the sea, and over the fowl of the air, and over every living thing that moveth upon the earth.

And God said, Behold, I have given you every herb bearing seed, which *is* upon the face of all the earth, and every tree, in the which *is* the fruit of a tree yielding seed; to you it shall be for meat.

And to every beast of the earth, and to every fowl of the air, and to every thing that creepeth upon the earth, wherein *there is* life, I *have given* every green herb for meat: and it was so.

Genesis 1:28-30

When God gave the name of Babel to man, they received power and authority to rule over both man and beast. Man used this power to make creatures, plants, and trees domestic, and to develop civilizations and kingdoms.

How and why were ancient works accomplished?

All around the world ancient man built many amazing works. Stone Hedge, the works on Easter Island, Indian mounds in Ohio and elsewhere, the Spinks, and pyramids around the world are just a few of these ancient works. Could they have been seeking a name from God by the way of the lesser light to rule over crops, animals, people, and maybe even the weather?

Considering the rise of civilization around these amazing ancient building projects, I would not be surprised to learn that many of these great works led to them receiving power and authority from God, or name.

Truly, ancient works are amazing. Where did primitive people receive the knowledge to accomplish such deeds?

I hypothesis that Satan, in the form of the great red dragon after he was removed from heaven, gave knowledge in the form of visions to either/or shamans and kings of these ancient people (Revelation 12:7-9). My guess is based on multiple and diverse stories of dragons throughout the world.

Does "ears to hear" create denominations within the church?

There are many divisions in the church because there are so many different beliefs and understandings concerning the interpretation of the Bible.

Why do you think there are so many different interpretations of the Bible? Why do Christians have so many different beliefs and understandings of what they think the Bible means? Even within each denomination there exists great differences in the Christian walk of life.

There are members in each denomination who have great love for God and feel God's love for them, while many others among the same belief long to have a stronger love for God and to feel God's love for them. Then there are also those in each denomination that have great faith and seem to have little difficulty getting their prayers answered, while many others struggle. It is true that lifestyles and sin have a large effect on our prayer life and faith outcome, but that doesn't explain why countless numbers of believers within each denomination who live their lives to please God don't get their prayers answered.

Have you ever wondered how some people can read the Bible and believe what is written while others can read it and not believe what is written? One might say it is God who reveals Himself to some but not to others, but if this is true, how does He choose to whom He will reveal Himself? Wouldn't this make God a respecter of persons?

I have presented many puzzling questions concerning how one comes to believe and understand God's written Word. How do Christians find answers to questions like these? What they should do is to pray first and then search the Scriptures with an open heart.

Jesus always spoke to the people in parables (Matthew 13:34). It is written that Jesus spoke to the people in parables because if He spoke to them without parables they would understand what He spoke, believe what He said, and then be saved (Mark 4:10-12). But why wouldn't Jesus want people to be saved? It wasn't that Jesus didn't want the people to be saved, but it was for their sake and for the sake of others that He wanted them to do other things first.

After Jesus spoke to the people in parables, He would say, "He that hath ears to hear let him hear." Obviously Jesus was not speaking of physical ears, so what could He have meant by the words "ears to hear?" What did the people need to have in order for them to hear Jesus or understand His words?

> And saying, The time is fulfilled, and the kingdom of God is at hand: repent ye, and believe the gospel.
>
> Mark 1:15

Jesus wanted the people to repent first, believe second, and then be saved. The preceding order allowed people to have power in the Kingdom of God while they were still alive here on the earth. Jesus wanted the people to have power of the Kingdom of God in order to help themselves and others to receive victories in this life.

Are you a Christian? Could you use more victories in your life? If so, you will appreciate the following information concerning repenting of sin, believing the Word of God, and understanding the written Word.

When people repent of their sins and ask God to forgive them, God forgives them at the time they ask for forgiveness. So why do so many of us feel like God hasn't really forgiven us of our sins?

In the Kingdom of God we must first give away what we want to receive. For example, God gave His Son to die for our sins and rise again in order for Him to receive many sons and daughters. When we ask for and receive forgiveness of our sins, this transaction happens between God and the person who He is forgiving, and it takes place in the spiritual world. To receive forgiveness in our physical world, we must give the forgiveness we received from God to others. This is accomplished by confessing our sins to others and proclaiming to others that God has forgiven us of our sins. We must also forgive those who have hurt us in the past.

I don't believe God is demanding us to confess specific sins, but He does want us to confess that we are sinners. Satan wants the world to believe we must confess every detail of our transgressions, but don't believe him. God knows everything we have done, and others don't need to know the details unless we are led by God to tell them in order to help them. Sometimes we are able to help others better if we have gone through the same experience ourselves.

At least three things happen when we obey God concerning repenting. First of all, others receive a spirit of repentance from God through us, which convicts them of their sins. Secondly, these people who obey God concerning repenting will feel the forgiveness of God, and their lives are changed for the better. Then lastly, they will receive ears to hear the Word of God.

Ears to hear are spirits, which help us to believe and understand the Word of God. To believe the Word of God we must understand it. To understand the Word of God we must believe it, but this is truly an impossible situation without ears to hear. Without repentance you will not receive ears to hear.

As Christians we must confess we believe the Word of God and then share with others what we understand about the written Word. In doing this, others will receive spirits to believe and understand the Word of God as they hear or read it.

The more we believe the written Word, the more we will understand it. The more we share with others what we understand about the written Word the more understanding we will receive.

> Take heed therefore how ye hear: for whosoever hath, to him shall be given; and whosoever hath not, from him shall be taken even that which he seemeth to have.
>
> Luke 8:18

For Jesus' kingdom on the earth to grow, people need to repent and share their repentance with others, believe and share their belief with others, and understand and share their understanding with others.

Is there something missing in your Christian walk with God? If so, following the above list will bring home what is missing.

We Christians need to have a balanced walk with God. Please don't be like I was for many years. After God called me and gave me a spirit to understand Genesis, I received a tremendous hunger for knowledge about creation.

My wife repeatedly warned me that I needed to work on my love walk and serving others. Even though I knew without a doubt that she was right, I spent most of my time, money, and energy seeking the truth about man's beginnings.

I lacked love for God because I didn't give the forgiveness God had given to me back to others by confessing my sins and telling others what God had done for me.

My faith walk was a mess. I believed the Bible concerning God's blessings for others, but I lacked the faith I needed to receive blessings from God for myself and for my family, even though we tithed and made offerings to God.

I failed to routinely confess to others that I believed the Word of God was true, that we believed God had blessed us at the time we prayed and asked for blessings, and that we were expecting to receive God's blessings in this life. I wanted to wait until we received blessings in this world before I confessed that God had blessed us. I didn't understand that we first receive blessings in the spiritual world, then we next confess the blessings we want to receive, and then we receive these blessings in this world.

Thank God I finally yielded to my wife's advice. I only wish I had listened to her sooner.

Please be balanced in your repenting, believing, and understanding. Make sure you give to others what God has given to you, for this is the way to have a joyful and abundant life.

In order for us to come to a point of repentance, we need to receive a spirit of repentance.

John the Baptist was born in the spirit and power of Elijah in order to prepare a people for the coming of Jesus (Matthew 3:1-3). The spirit of Elijah upon John the Baptist convicted the people of their sins. After they repented of their sins and were baptized in water, the people were also able to pass on the spirit and power of Elijah to others through the Holy Spirit.

All Christians have a spirit of repentance to some degree of fullness depending upon what the Spirit of God gives to each of us. All Christians also have a spirit of believing to some degree of fullness. Based upon the fact that God had Ezekiel bear the iniquity of Israel and Judah, I believe Jesus used Ezekiel's name spirit when He was in the flesh. God also repeatedly called Ezekiel the son of man, and Jesus called Himself the Son of Man.

Finally, I believe all Christians have a spirit of understanding to some degree of fullness, which are the spirit and the power of Daniel in the Old Testament. I believe Paul had the spirit and the power of Daniel. I base this belief on Daniel's lifestyle, his ability to interpret dreams, his deep understanding of the written Word, and the amount of and the kind of communication he had with God. Certainly God gave Paul a spirit of understanding, which he needed in order to write most of the New Testament that God revealed to him.

People with like beliefs, concerning fullness of spirit of repentance, believing, and understanding, come together to form denominations within the church. People naturally prefer to be around others who think and feel like they do.

Christians should seek to obey the Holy Spirit by repenting, believing, and understanding, not just in the particular spirit where they have the most fullness of spirit. We the body of Christ must endeavor not to be out of balance. Most importantly, we must have patience and understanding with denominations that have different fullness of spirits than our own denomination has.

I do not want to use the names of denominations so I will present my view in a different way. For example, Republicans should endeavor to be like Democrats as much as their fullness of spirit will allow them, and the same should be true for the Democrats. They should earnestly try to understand the Republicans' point of view and seek cooperation whenever possible. The same is true for the body of Christ. We need love, respect, and cooperation between the denominations.

Old Testament prophets Elijah, Ezekiel, and Daniel received name spirits, or spirit and power, for the work they did for God while on the earth. John the Baptist, Jesus, and Paul received the name spirits of these dead prophets through the Holy Spirit, which they used to do the will of God and to anoint others to do the will of God.

I also believe that Peter, James, and John received name spirit or spirit and power upon their deaths, which are available today for the repentance of sin, the believing of the written Word, and the understanding of the written Word. They received their name spirit for obeying God when God spoke the words "This is my beloved Son: hear him" (Mark 9:7). The words God spoke to Peter, James, and John on the Mount of Transfiguration gave them the ability to obey God in repenting, believing, and understanding.

Every Christian will receive name spirit based on their obedience to the Word of God while on the earth (Revelation 2:17). Countless numbers of others will use and obey our name spirits in order to receive name spirit of their own after they die. This is the power over the nations that Jesus promised to overcomers.

> And he that overcometh, and keepeth my works unto the end, to him I will give power over the nations:
>
> Revelation 2:26

In conclusion, denominations within the church are the result of individuals who have received different amounts of fullness of spirit in the areas of repentance, believing, and understanding. Regardless of the fullness of spirit the Holy Spirit has given each of us, God wants us to obey Him in all areas. The fullness of spirit you presently have represents who you are now, not who you should become. Grow and become strong in the Lord by obeying the Lord.

Seeker's Gold

If a quarterback throws a pass right-handed, chances are good that his next pass will be right-handed also. As a matter of fact, he probably threw right-handed before you even saw him throw. When seeking information on how God created man, wouldn't it be wise to look at the way he is now creating a new species of man?

God is presently creating a new species of man for himself. Members of the son-of-man species are being changed into the son-of-God species.

> Therefore if any man *be* in Christ, *he is* a *new creature*: old things are passed away; behold, all things are become new.
>
> II Corinthians 5:17
> [*last emphasis* added]

> But as many as received him, to them gave he power to become the sons of God, *even* to them that believe on his name:
>
> John 1:12

At the present time, the Lord God is working on the minds and hearts of believers in Jesus Christ. Sometime in the future, God will give them heavenly bodies. That's the way he is doing it now, and that's the way he did it way back when he created man here in the earth.

Man of the Garden of Eden obeyed the voice of Satan and received the fruit, which caused him to die from the Day of Man and to be born into the Day of the Creature. Obeying the voice of Jesus causes believers to receive the fruits that cause believers to die from this present day and be born into the Day of Jesus Christ in Heaven. Anyone who receives Jesus Christ as their Lord and Savior receives a new spirit and a new heart within their spirit being. Man's old heart and spirit could not hold the new wine of the Holy Spirit.

Before people could receive Jesus' words when He was here in the earth, they had to have ears to hear. That is, they needed to have a mind that was anointed to understand Jesus' words.

John the Baptist's words were anointed. John anointed those who repented of their sins and were baptized so they could hear (understand) the words of Jesus. It was the blood of Abel that carried the anointing of Adam to the early people in order for them to have the ears to hear the word of man.

Thanks to Abel, the early people received the ability to hear (understand) the words of Cain. Cain's words were anointed with the name of Adam to cause the creatures to develop higher souls.

Early people with developed man souls could receive Seth as anointed word of man from Day Six. Seth's anointing caused early people to develop hearts of man. Early man could then call upon the name of God. God gave them the name of Adam to set them free from their old animal selves so they could become members of the son-of-man species.

By the way of the lesser light, God gave the son-of-man species seven name-spirit covenants. The first name spirit covenant was called "Babel" which came at the time the people, who built a city and a tower, knitted their souls and hearts together to make a name. The other six name-spirit covenants were Egypt, Assyria, Babylon, Persia, Greece, and Rome. Power and authority that flowed through these seven name spirits gave members of the son-of-man species the ability to create kingdoms and to rule over nations.

By the way of the greater light, God also gave the son-of-man species another set of name-spirit covenants. The name Adam was the first name spirit given to man and then to the son-of-man species. It was removed at the time of the Flood. The name-spirit covenants of Noah, Abraham, Israel, Moses, David, and Jesus were next.

God used the seven name spirits from the greater light to bring forth Jesus in the flesh. Jesus died on the cross and rose on the third day. After forty days, He went back to heaven, and then the Father sent back the Holy Spirit to believers of Jesus Christ

Because of the work Jesus did on the cross and the martyrdom of His believers, Satan as the red dragon was removed from heaven and placed in the sea, which is one part of the earth's spirit realm. The beast that rose out of the sea and the beast that rose out of the earth were both forms of Satan, like Jesus and the Holy Spirit are forms of the Father.

Jesus and the Holy Spirit did the will of the Father for the good of mankind. The beast out of the sea and the beast out of the earth did the will of Satan, which is to do evil to mankind.

Those who yield to Jesus and the Holy Spirit will have companionship with Jesus in the New Jerusalem, which is in the New Heaven. Those who yield to evil spirits from the beast will have companionship with Satan in the lake of fire

About seventeen years ago, I was a man who needed to know the truth about God. With a broken heart and an open mind I asked God to lead me to the truth.

God revealed many things to me. He taught me how to look past understandings already in my mind and to search the Scriptures until deeper truths were revealed.

God showed me that in order to receive better understandings I had to be willing to set aside my old beliefs. Sometimes these were understandings that took me years to receive.

You have stayed the course to the end. That tells me you too have an open mind and are hungry for the truth. Truly, you are a seeker. I will make one last plea. Don't let this book be a finish line. Make it a starting point. Search the Scriptures, as only a seeker can do, with an open mind and an open heart.

Seekers know wisdom is more precious than gold. An open mind is a bucket to receive wisdom.

God bless.

Appendix A
Creation Days

The following chart depicts the three parts of each creation day's evening, morning, and seed light.

Manifestations of God's Spoken Word
—Let There Be—

Evening	Morning	Seed Light
Darkness	Light	Divided light
Waters	Firmament	Divided waters
Gathered waters	Dry land	Plants
1st lights (greater - lesser)	2nd lights (blessing)	3rd lights (upon earth)
Living creature (moving creature-fowl)	Blessing	Earth's living creature (upon earth) (spoken on 6th day)
Man (male-female)	1st dominion blessing	2nd dominion blessing for food
God (on-in)	Blessed (7th day)	Sanctified 7th day (divided from other days)

The italicized words belong to the days where the "Let there be" statements are not found in the Bible but are believed to have been spoken, or spoken without the words "Let there be."

Appendix B
Promises Within Names

The following chart depicts the names God gave to His creations and the promises that came within each name.

Receiver	Name	Promise
Face of waters	Spirit of God	Darkness Light Divided light
Void	*Spirit of God*	Waters Firmament Divided waters
Light	Day	7th evening (rested) 7th morning (blessed) Sanctified
Darkness	Night	Gathered waters Dry *land* Plants
Firmament	Heaven	Lights (greater & lesser) Lights (signs & seasons) Light upon earth
Dry *land*	Earth	Man (male & female) 1st Dominion blessing 2nd Dominion blessing for food
Gathered waters	Seas	Moving creature & fowl Blessing Earth's living creatures

The italicized "Spirit of God" was not mentioned in the first chapter of Genesis but I believe it was present at the creation of the waters.

Appendix C
Levels of Creation

First Level of Creation

Day Seven (Kingdom of God)

Day One (light) morning

————————————

Second Level of Creation

Day Four (Kingdom of Lights/Kingdom of Heaven)
greater – lesser light

Day Two (firmament) morning

————————————

Third Level of Creation

Day Six (kingdom of man)
man – woman

Day Five (kingdom of creatures)
moving creatures – fowl

Day Three dry (*land*)
gathered waters (wet)

Bibliography

Aimov, Isaac. *Asimov's New Guide to Science.* New York: Basic Books, Inc., 1984.

Godfrey, Laurie R. *Scientist Confront Creationism.* New York – London: W. W. Norton and Company, 1984.

Gribbin, John. *Almost Everyone's Guide to Science.* New Haven and London: Yale University Press, 1999.

Jones, Roger S. *Physics for the Rest of Us.* Lincolnwood (Chicago), Illinois: Contemporary Books, 1992.

Mayr, Ernst. *What Evolution Is.* New York: Basic Books, 2001.

Ronan, Colin A. (ed.). *Science Explained.* New York: Henry Holt and Company, 1993.

Rothaman, Tony. *Instant Physics.* Fawcitt Columbine, NewYork: Byron Press Book, 1995.

WGBH Educational Foundation and Clear Blue Sky Productions, Inc. *The Common Genetic Code,* <http://www.pbs.org/wgbhevolution/library/04/4/1_044_02.html> (1999).

Woese, Carl. *Intimate Strangers Unseen Life on Earth,* <http://www.pbs.org/opb/intimatestrangers/treeoflife/index.html> (1999).

Zannoni, Arthur E. (ed.). *Jews and Christians Speak of Jesus.* Minneapolis: Fortress Press, 1994

End Notes

1 For with God nothing shall be impossible. (Luke 1:37)

2 So when they had dined, Jesus saith to Simon Peter, Simon, *son* of Jonas, lovest thou me more than these? He saith unto him, Yea, Lord; thou knowest that I love thee. He saith unto him, Feed my lambs. He saith to him again the second time, Simon, *son* of Jonas, lovest thou me? He saith unto him, Yea, Lord; thou knowest that I love thee. He saith unto him, Feed my sheep. He saith unto him the third time, Simon, *son* of Jonas, lovest thou me? Peter was grieved because he said unto him the third time, Lovest thou me? And he said unto him, Lord, thou knowest all things; thou knowest that I love thee. Jesus saith unto him, Feed my sheep. (John 21:15-17)

3 And saw heaven opened, and a certain vessel descending unto him, as it had been a great sheet knit at the four corners, and let down to the earth: Wherein were all manner of fourfooted beasts of the earth, and wild beasts, and creeping things, and fowls of the air. And there came a voice to him, Rise, Peter; kill, and eat. But Peter said, Not so, Lord; for I have never eaten any thing that is common or unclean. And the voice *spake* unto him again the second time, What God hath cleansed, *that* call not thou common. This was done thrice: and the vessel was received up again into heaven. (Acts 10:11-16)

4 And Jesus said unto them, Because of your unbelief: for verily I say unto you, If ye have faith as a grain of mustard seed, ye shall say unto this mountain, Remove hence to yonder place; and it shall remove; and nothing shall be impossible unto you. (Matthew 17:20)

5 All things were made by him; and without him was not any thing made that was made. (John 1:3)

6 Jesus answered and said unto her, Whosoever drinketh of this water shall thirst again: But whosoever drinketh of the water that I shall give him shall never thirst; but the water that I shall give him shall be in him a well of water springing up into everlasting life. (John 4:13-14)

7 And he saith unto me, The waters which thou sawest, where the whore sitteth, are peoples, and multitudes, and nations, and tongues. (Revelation 17:15)

8 It is the spirit that quickeneth; the flesh profiteth nothing: the words that I speak unto you, *they* are spirit, and *they* are life. (John 6:63)

9 And I beheld, and, lo, in the midst of the throne and of the four beasts, and in the midst of the elders, stood a Lamb as it had been slain, having seven horns and seven eyes, which are the seven Spirits of God sent forth into all the earth. (Revelation 5:6)

10 All the while my breath *is* in me, and the spirit of God *is* in my nostrils; (Job 27:3)

11 And the eyes of them both were opened, and they knew that they were *naked*; and they sewed fig leaves together, and made themselves aprons. (Genesis 3:7)

12 And God said, Let us make man in our image, after our likeness: and let them have dominion over the fish of the sea, and over the fowl of the air, and over the cattle, and over all the earth, and over every creeping thing that creepeth upon the earth. (Genesis 1:26)

13 Thou *art* the anointed cherub that covereth; and I have set thee *so*: thou wast upon the holy mountain of God; thou hast walked up and down in the midst of the stones of fire. (Ezekiel 28:14)

14 I am the living bread which came down from heaven: if any man eat of this bread, he shall live for ever: and the bread that I will give is my flesh, which I will give for the life of the world. The Jews therefore strove among themselves, saying, How can this man give us *his* flesh to eat? Then Jesus said unto them, Verily, verily, I say unto you, Except ye eat the flesh of the Son of man, and drink his blood, ye have no life in you. Whoso eateth my flesh, and drinketh my blood, hath eternal life; and I will raise him up at the last day. For my flesh is meat indeed, and my blood is drink indeed. He that eateth my flesh, and drinketh my blood, dwelleth in me, and I in him. As the living Father hath sent me, and I live by the Father: so he that eateth me, even he shall live by me. This is that bread which came down from heaven: not as your fathers did eat manna, and are dead: he that eateth of this bread shall live for ever. (John 6:51-58)

15 But flesh with the life thereof, *which is* the blood thereof, shall ye not eat. (Genesis 9:4)

16 And Adam knew his wife again; and she bare a son, and called his name Seth: For God, *said she*, hath appointed me another seed instead of Abel, whom Cain slew. (Genesis 4:25)

17 Therefore *it is* of faith, that it *might be* by grace; to the end the promise might be sure to all the seed; not to that only which is of the law, but to that also which is of the faith of Abraham; who is the father of us all, (Romans 4:16)

18 Who, being in the form of God, thought it not robbery to be equal with God: But made himself of no reputation, and took upon him the

179

form of a servant, and was made in the likeness of men: (Philippians 2:6-7)

19 When Pharaoh shall speak unto you, saying, Shew a miracle for you: then thou shalt say unto Aaron, Take thy rod, and cast *it* before Pharaoh, *and* it shall become a serpent. And Moses and Aaron went in unto Pharaoh, and they did so as the Lord had commanded: and Aaron cast down his rod before Pharaoh, and before his servants, and it became a serpent. (Exodus 7:9-10)

20 And think not to say within yourselves, We have Abraham to *our* father: for I say unto you, that God is able of these stones to raise up children unto Abraham. (Matthew 3:9)

21 And it shall come to pass in that day, I will hear, saith the Lord, I will hear the heavens, and they shall hear the earth; (Hosea 2:21)

22 I Jesus have sent mine angel to testify unto you these things in the churches. I am the root and the offspring of David, *and* the bright and morning star. (Revelation 22:16)

23 And he that overcometh, and keepeth my works unto the end, to him will I give power over the nations: And he shall rule them with a rod of iron; as the vessels of a potter shall they be broken to shivers: even as I received of my Father. And I will give him the morning star. (Revelation 2:26-28)

24 And the Lord God said, *It is* not good that the man should be alone; I will make him an help meet for him. And out of the ground the Lord God formed every beast of the field, and every fowl of the air; and brought *them* unto Adam to see what he would call them: and whatsoever Adam called every living creature, that *was* the name thereof. And Adam gave names to all cattle, and to the fowl of the air, and to every beast of the field; but for Adam there was not found an help meet for him. (Genesis 2:18-20)

25 Awake, awake, put on strength, O arm of the Lord; awake, as in ancient days, in the generation of old. *Art* thou not it that hath cut Rahab, *and* wounded the dragon? *Art* thou not it which hath dried the sea, the waters the great deep; that hath made the depths of the sea a way for the ransomed to pass over? (Isaiah 51:9-10)

26 And the men of Judah came, and there they anointed David king over the house of Judah. And they told David, saying, *That* the men of Jabeshgilead *were they* that buried Saul. (II Samuel 2:4)

After this I beheld, and lo another, like a leopard, which had upon the back of it four wings of a fowl; the beast had also four heads; and dominion was given to it. (Daniel 7:6)

27 And unto the angel of the church in Sardis write; These things saith he that hath the seven Spirits of God, and the seven stars; I know thy works, that thou hast a name that thou livest, and art dead. (Revelation 3:1)

28 Wherefore God also hath highly exalted him, and given him a name which is above every name: That at the name of Jesus every knee should bow, of *things* in heaven, and *things* in earth, and *things* under the earth; (Philippians 2:9-10)

29 Not as Cain, *who* was of that wicked one, and slew his brother. And wherefore slew he him? Because his own works were evil, and his brother's righteous. (I John 3:12)

For the promise, that he should be the heir of the world, *was* not to Abraham, or to his seed, through the law, but through the righteousness of faith. For if they which are of the law *be* heirs, faith is made void, and the promise made of none effect: Because the law worketh wrath: for where no law is, *there is* no transgression. Therefore *it is* of faith, that *it might be* by grace; to the end the promise might be sure to all the seed; not to that only which is of the law, but to that also which is of the faith of Abraham; who is the father of us all, (Romans 4:13-16)

30 And so it is written, The first man Adam was made a living soul; the last Adam *was made* a quickening spirit. (I Corinthians 15:45)

31 And he said, Therefore said I unto you, that no man can come unto me, except it were given unto him of my Father. (John 6:65)

32 Nevertheless I tell you the truth; It is expedient for you that I go away: for if I go not away, the Comforter will not come unto you; but if I depart, I will send him unto you. (John 16:7)

33 And the Lord God said unto the serpent, Because thou hast done this, thou *art* cursed above all cattle, and above every beast of the field; upon thy belly shalt thou go, and dust shalt thou eat all the days of thy life: (Genesis 3:14)

34 It is sown a natural body; it is raised a spiritual body. There is a natural body, and there is a spiritual body. (I Corinthians 15:44)

35 And I saw the dead, small and great, stand before God; and the books were opened: and another book was opened, which is *the book* of life: and the dead were judged out of those things which were written in the books, according to their works. And the sea gave up the dead which were in it; and death and hell delivered up the dead which were in them: and they were judged every man according to their works. And death and hell were cast into the lake of fire. This is the second death. And whosoever was not found written in the book of life was cast into the lake of fire. (Revelation 20:12-15)

Index

V

W

Printed in the United States
61878LVS00002B/189